Tails Are Wagging on Crete

A True Story,
Our Cretan Journey with Animals

By Freida Richards

Eloquent Books
New York, New York

Eloquent Books

An imprint of AEG Publishing Group

845 Third Avenue, 6th Floor - 6016

New York, NY 10022

www.eloquentbooks.com

ISBN 978-1-60860-569-9

Printed in the United States of America

Illustrations: Pamela Williams

Book Design: Linda W. Rigsbee

"The soul is the same in all living creatures,
although the body of each is different."
—Hippocrates, Greek Physician

Dedication

I WOULD LIKE to dedicate this book firstly to my dear husband Colin, who has also worked tirelessly since the day we arrived and whose practical genius has never failed to amaze me.

Without his total commitment to animals, we could not have continued, and without his abilities, none of us would have roofs over our heads.

Secondly I would like to dedicate it to my dear veterinarian George Vizyrakis, who I would like to thank for his constant inspiration and generosity of spirit and for teaching me so much over the years about the care of sick and injured animals.

To the many volunteers, and especially to Alison Bullen who has helped me over the past seven years in all aspects of the work.

Also to the *Protectors of Animals* all over the world.

Acknowledgements

TO PAMELA WILLIAMS, with grateful thanks for her sensitive and generous contribution of artwork throughout the book.

To Nicol Milburn (qualified veterinary nurse), for her information and contributions on the treatment of animal poisoning.

To Ted Davison, for his patience with my constant bombarding of questions about Information Technology.

All the proceeds from the sale of this book will go toward animal welfare on Crete.

Contents

One | In the Beginning

IF ANYONE IS to be held responsible for my current unorthodox lifestyle, I tell my three now adult children, it is Richard Briers, Felicity Kendal, and the producers of the television program "The Good Life." I can still recall my feelings of euphoria at the beginning of every episode and my disappointment at the end of them, only to be relieved by the prospect of another episode to be shown the following week. As a young mother in my mid-twenties living in Beckenham in South East London with three children all under the age of five years, and with a love of the countryside and the good life, how I longed to return to my country roots.

I was born in North Yorkshire, the youngest of four girls, who were all a great deal older than myself, so for the first ten years of my life, I was sent away at every opportunity to stay with my eldest married sister and her husband on their farm. I can remember endless, hot, sunny days at harvest time helping my sister to pack up the farm laborers' lunch and taking it to the field. I have vivid memories of romping through hayfields and eating cheese and tomato sandwiches in the shade of an old oak tree in the heat of the day with my back pressed firmly against its gnarled and twisted trunk. I had the luxury of drinking the diluted orange squash (it had a special taste for those of you that can remember—strong and very sweet; it was the orange squash that was provided by the National Health Service in England just after the war, sold very cheaply at the weekly baby clinics) straight from the bottle. Then when the day's work had been completed, I recall, as if it was only yesterday, riding home on top of the old hay wagon, which was pulled by a creamy-coloured Clydesdale by the name of Snowball. The sheer thrill and excitement mingled with the fear of sitting aloft on the freshly cut hay, which has a smell like no other, a fresh, intoxicating aroma that has stayed with me all my life. Even today when I smell the scent of newly cut grass, I am so easily transported back to North Yorkshire and to the child of about five years of age being thrown from side to side as Snowball stepped out, eager to get home as the old cart rattled and creaked and rumbled its way over the rough lanes back to the farmhouse.

I harbor memories of feeding motherless lambs from pint, glass, milk bottles that had huge rubber teats tied to their necks and being transfixed and amazed at the newborn lambs' incredible strength as they sucked greedily at the teat, my small hands barley able to keep a grasp of the huge round bottle as they tugged and pulled and guzzled greedily at the warm creamy milk.

But there I was in the early 1970s, like the Goods living in suburbia, with the only difference being my three small children and a husband whose only connection to the countryside was the catgut on his guitar and the hops in his beer! Back then I had about as much chance of living my dream as Gerald and Marjorie had of persuading Tom and Barbara to give up their newfound way of living or of Tom and Barbara getting Gerald and Marjorie to join them in the good life. As the years passed, my energies were channelled into raising my three wonderful children, but deep in my soul I never lost the urge to return to the simpler, natural way of life.

Well, here I am now about thirty-five years later, living on the beautiful island of Crete, with another husband who shares my love of the countryside, animals, and all aspects of wildlife.

The tales in this book began with our purchasing a piece of agricultural land measuring approximately three acres, or ten *stremma* in Greek terms, and living—with no electricity–two kilometers from our nearest neighbor. In a house not yet completed, we shared our lives with our two horses, six sheep, numerous chickens, one very elderly donkey, thirty-three cats, and seven dogs of our own, and in addition to those at any given time we housed between thirty and forty abandoned puppies, several adult homeless dogs, three rabbits, and two ferrets. With very little spare cash, we managed in those early days to start a dog and cat hotel, and with Colin being an excellent carpenter, he soon found plenty of work. So for us, it is our way of living "The Good Life."

Like so many people who make dramatic life changes, our plans did not turn out as we hoped. We had always known that before arriving here, we would need to find employment. I had a vague notion that I would learn the Greek language during the first year and find employment in some sort of social work capacity or in a hospital. How very naive I was back in those early days. For anyone over the age of fifty who has tried to learn the Greek language will understand just how naive I was because seven years later, I am still struggling to learn Greek. Back then I somehow forgot that my brain was not as agile as it was thirty years ago when I was living in Holland and learning to speak Dutch. Neither was I aware of just how difficult the Greek language is for us Northern Europeans to learn.

Nor had we expected to be ripped off financially by the Greek real estate agent and builder, who we trusted implicitly. Living here now, we realize that to expect total honesty from a Cretan in any business venture is unrealistic in a country where even a brother tells you that he would not trust his own brother. Ripping off other people is in the blood of far too many; I am sorry to say. "Beware of Greeks bearing gifts" springs to mind. The Cretans for sure will tell you what you want to hear, and even if it's a downright lie, they see no wrong in it. Had we known this in the beginning, then a lot of the problems that we encountered could have been avoided. But with all the problems and pitfalls—and believe me there have been many, and not only pitfalls but landslides—I cannot ever imagine returning to live in England. Hopefully the contents of this book will help you to understand why. "So how did you manage to get yourself into this position?" I can hear you saying, and I think the best person to explain the situation to you would be Arnold.

Two | Arnold's Tail

PLEASE ALLOW ME to introduce myself. I am a dark, bay, warm-blooded hunter standing just a little more than seventeen two hands, that is, and a mere twenty-three years young. I am very handsome, the sort of equine who can make heads turn. My father's name was Dutch Courage, and he was a British dressage champion, a fact of which I am eminently proud. (They attempted to point me in that direction—you know, like father like son and all that—but I had other careers in mind.) My full name is Drastic Measures, but I am known as Arnie to my closest friends and Arnold when I am not in Freida's and Colin's good books. Currently I am living here in Apokoronas, Western Crete, with my companion Prince, a rather eccentric (how I would very much like to say neurotic) ex-show jumper. At the age of thirty–seven, he is probably the oldest horse on Crete and quite possibly the oldest horse in Greece. According to a census taken back in 1928, Crete had six thousand horses, ten thousand mules, and forty thousand donkeys, but where they all are today, I shudder to think. So what are we doing on Crete, of all places, and how did we manage to get here? You may well ask.

The tale starts about ten years ago when Colin and Freida, our owners, decided to take a holiday on this beautiful island. After several more holidays, and having fallen head over heels in love with the place, they planned to move here lock, stock, and barrel. Animal lovers through and through, they spent many long hours trying to find good and permanent homes for their pet sheep, chickens, and ducks. If they could have transported them too, then they would have done so. Believe me; they tried! It was tough planning the move for dear old Prince and myself. It would appear that no one had ever taken horses as far as Crete before. Some transporters whom Freida contacted were not prepared to take an old man like Prince on such a long and stressful journey. I suppose they thought that he just might pop his horseshoes!

Part of any arrangement had to be that Colin and Freida travelled alongside us, not trusting anyone else to care for us on such a long trip; that's the sort of people they are. They eventually discovered a wonderful company called Shelly Ashman, who agreed to get us all from Kent, England, to Crete, Greece, in one week. After endless visits from the vet and the equine dentist and Colin's crash course in shoeing from our farrier Wayne, we were ready to leave. The documentation was endless; even the two ferrets had a clean bill of health from the vet.

Finally, the big day arrived. Colin and Freida and friends bandaged eight legs and wrapped our tails; mine is rather long and thick and lustrous, even if I do say so myself, and it can become a lethal weapon if one is pushed. They made me wear the most hideous headgear, which was not very becoming for an equine of my stature, rather like a padded cap with two holes for my ears, the sort of thing that you might put on a donkey. The problem was that it kept on slipping sideways, which made me look rather like I had just emerged from an all-night party, rather the worse for wear. I was just pleased that none of my hunting chums were there to see me, or I would have been the laughing stock of next season. We had been washed and clipped and groomed and shod, we gleamed like two shiny new euros, and we had been given rather smart, new travel rugs to wear.

Jannie, who was to be our excellent carer for the next seven days, arrived with his two helpers at our stables in Kent in the southeast of England early in the morning. It was a bit too early for Colin, who it seems, had rather one too many farewell nights at his local pub, The Crown in nearby Edenbridge. As a result, he and Freida were obviously not on speaking terms as we prepared to depart. Being as accustomed as I am to travel with my previous owner, I led Prince into the most enormous, modern, roomy, and air-conditioned horse trailer, where seventeen other fellow equines were already ensconced, all young chaps, but civil enough. Two were bound for France and the rest for Northern Greece; they told me. I think we were getting the better deal knowing what I know now about the terrible treatment and neglect that many of my fellow equines have been subjected to in both of those destinations. Meanwhile, Freida and Colin hitched up their rather old and dilapidated four-berth camper, which was to be their home for several months to come, to their pickup truck. Their precious black-and-white cat and two ferrets were safely positioned inside their mobile home (for the time being anyway). The pickup truck, which was to house their five large dogs sitting in the back under a tin roof, was steered into position.

My goodness, the stress levels were at a peak that day; everyone was crying and saying farewell to Colin and Freida and, of course, Prince and myself. The dogs were all in a panic, lest they were left behind, and eagerly leapt onto the back of the truck not having a clue of course of just what lay ahead of them, so like dogs! Really, in hindsight, it was only old Prince and myself who held it all together, and he, being a rather highly strung creature, was lucky to have someone like me to go along with him. He knows that I always take the lead and set an example. It's the breeding, you know; it shows every time.

Our first stop was Dover where we caught the ferry to Calais. The law states quite firmly that we equines have to be given water every four hours, so that meant regular stops along the way. Once we were in France, the trailer thundered along the excellent motorways with Colin driving in hot pursuit. The old camper was swaying and creaking in an attempt to keep up with the procession until we finally arrived late that evening at our first stopover. It was the famous Chantilly racecourse just outside Paris. What a relief it was to leave the trailer and put all four feet on terra firma again; I can tell you. Every equine was exercised by Jannie and his staff, assisted by Colin. We were all given supper and bedded down for the night in very comfortable and clean stables with a sumptuous supply of clean, fresh straw. Bandages were removed from legs, and tails were unwrapped. I delighted in a good roll and slept extremely well with old Prince nearby. By this time the dogs were again showing signs of their intense insecurity for fear of being left somewhere that they did not recognise, and they were all seen clambering to get into the small camper, but after a brief walk, I have to report that all five stayed amazingly close to heel, the like of which I never witnessed before. They were fed and tethered to the camper and eagerly settled down for the night in the sure knowledge that their master and mistress were ensconced inside.

For Freida and Colin, the journey felt surreal at times. Leaving one's homeland is never an easy decision to make, and yet they both felt that the England they had known and loved and grown up in, sadly, no longer existed. They had both worked hard all their lives, and really all they now wanted to do was to live a peaceful and quiet life, maybe to build a small bungalow on the ten acres of land they had purchased in Kent. But the local authority bylaws and petty bureaucracy had made this impossible. In fact even building a chicken shed seemed to be a logistical nightmare. (Yet, if you were prepared to break the law and trespass onto other people's property, the local authorities in England seemed to be able to give you all the support that you needed, supplying washing facilities and toilets and whatever else you required.) So Freida and Colin's decision was to move to a country where they felt that they could live the life they dreamed of. But when you have animals, and like Colin and Freida truly love and respect them, then this is not an easy decision to make. They knew that there really would be no going back.

The following morning we were all up before daylight, bandages replaced on seventeen horsy legs (I make that sixty-eight bandages in total), tails wrapped, and rugs fastened. Then after breakfast we were off again, the five dogs all eager to be the first one onto the back of the truck. (At the risk of repeating myself, I have to say it again. Insecure creatures, dogs; don't you think?) The poor old cat, otherwise known as Bill, I understood was already feeling rather traumatized after having been thrown around the camper as it swayed perilously from side to side in order to keep up with the truck. On to Lyon, Torino, Alessandria, and Cervia, stopping overnight at stables prebooked along the route by Jannie. The days were endless for us equines standing in one position. The worst day was probably the second one when we drove for over twelve hours with only brief stops for water, but Prince and I, being more mature and seasoned travellers than the youngsters onboard, did our best to keep up morale. Prince regaled us all with endless tales of how many riders he had unseated, usually headfirst into ponds and streams. His experiences were hilarious, like the time that he and Colin were being chased by the local police after someone had reported Colin for riding a horse in the dark without lights. (Prince told us all that was not true because he was wearing lights, but he was more worried about Colin being charged with being drunk in charge of a horse, so they four-legged it, so to speak, across country.) Prince told us he could always find his way home with or without a rider, and by all accounts, it was mostly without.

But the most amusing event of the entire journey, as far as I was concerned, was when the tailgate of Colin and Freida's truck fell down, just as they were entering the very long tunnel through the Alps from France to Italy. For some reason, the vehicle that we were travelling in was at the rear, and through my window I could see all those troublesome dogs hanging on for dear life lest they should be ejected as they were driven slowly up the steep incline to the entrance of the tunnel. The sight of those five nuisances sitting stiff legged with their backs pressed firmly against the cab, motionless and silent, was really making my day until some well-meaning truck driver pointed out the problem to Freida and Colin as they waited at the toll, and of course Freida leapt out and secured the tailgate, much to the relief of all its inhabitants.

You may have gathered at this point that I am not a great lover of dogs in general. That is because up until the time that I went to live with Freida, I had experienced the dreadful beasts yapping at my heels every week of my life as I led the Coakham Bloodhounds. Although we only chased humans in the latter years, it is still not something we talk about as Freida and Colin are strictly antihunting. But as I explained to them, I never had any choice in the matter. It was the life that I was born into, so to speak. What's more, neither Freida nor Colin nor I would ever hear a wrong word said against my previous owner Linda Thompson, who could be described as a slightly eccentric American woman and "Master of the Bloodhounds." If it were not for Linda, I would not be around today. She loved me and trained me and taught me all that I know and got me through some very difficult and painful, not to mention expensive, surgery. Many an owner would have had me shot at the mere sight of the bill let alone the dedication that it took to get me through the experience and fit again. Thank you, Linda.

From Rimini we headed for the ferry at Ancona. Jannie had made this long sea voyage many times before, and therefore he knew exactly what he was doing. He positioned the horse trailer on the top deck close to the rail to ensure that the fresh sea breeze would blast through, refreshing everyone and making the next sixteen hours of standing in one position almost bearable. Although by now Prince and I were really starting to feel the strain.

Things only got worse when we arrived at Patra, where we left most of our travelling companions. Prince and I were taken with four other equines on rather a long journey in order to drop them off on the other side of Athens. It was the evening before we reached our own stables in that city. The stables were not quite up to the usual standard of cleanliness to which we were accustomed—I am sorry to say—but I was feeling rather travel sick by now, and I just slumped. Freida and Colin were feeling rather guilty about the stress they had put us both through, and they spent their entire evening checking up on us, well, especially me.

By now the strain of the journey was telling on everyone. Colin insisted on doing all the driving, and the days had been long, and the nights had been short. Keeping all the animals fed and in good condition was Freida and Colin's main priority, along with coping in the restricted area of their small camper, where most of their belongings had by now fallen from wall to floor inside as the vehicle swayed and stopped and started, pulled along at speeds it clearly was not intended for. Now its neat and orderly contents were scattered everywhere, resembling the aftermath of a hurricane. Somewhere deep inside was the traumatized cat, who had managed to escape his confined area and was now hiding under the bed—and what's more, he preferred to remain there for the entire journey. Only the two ferrets appeared to be untouched by the experience and slept throughout.

Prince, on the other hoof, appeared to be coping much better than all of us. Whilst I was quite an attraction because of my good looks and size (of course my good looks have always made heads turn in my direction as I may have mentioned to you before, but it's just something that I have had to learn to live with), it would appear that seldom had these Greek horsy people seen such an elderly equine as Prince. The Greek children in particular kept looking at his teeth and patting us both. They were all rather astonished that anyone would own such an old horse let alone still ride him and enter him in shows. It would seem that once you reach the age of twenty here in Athens, then you're horsemeat, so to speak. Jannie had very thoughtfully booked us all at the stables for several nights, as he realized that we would benefit from a good few days rest and recuperation, and how right he was.

Freida and Colin had parked their camper on a piece of spare land next to the stables. After a day's rest Colin had the not-so-very-bright idea that it would do old Prince and I good to be walked the short distance from the stables to where they had set up camp, so Prince and I could stretch our legs and munch some of the grass. Unfortunately, being a newcomer to Greece, Colin did not realize that unlike England, there is seldom anywhere that has anything even remotely resembling a fence in the entire country.

Now I know that Prince won't mind my telling you that he had experienced a very traumatic early life with tales of ill treatment that you just would not want to hear about. That was of course before Colin found him. Due to this dreadful treatment during his formative years, Prince can behave, shall we say, a little unpredictably, so no one other than a Colin-type person would even consider owning him, let alone riding him. Prince is what is known in equine speak as "head shy." That means, if you put your hand or anything else up in the air even remotely near his head, he will rear up and take off at speed without giving any thought about the consequences of this action. Fear, you see, takes over, and then flight follows. He spooks at almost anything that he has not seen before and often at things that he has seen before. All in all, he is unpredictable, and to make matters even worse, he is impossible to catch and will never come when he is called. (Unlike me, who always comes when I am called, but there again, I have never known anything except love and kindness since I was a foal. Coming when I was called usually meant treats and not a good thrashing for doing nothing wrong.)

So there we were, for the first time in over a week getting the chance to taste the green, green grass of Athens, and what happened? Freida led Prince, and she stumbled on the wet muddy ground, instinctively raised her arms to save herself, and—yes, you've guessed it—Prince was off like a jet-propelled rocket. Chaos ensued, and I was unceremoniously rushed back to my stable without so much as a blade of grass passing my parched lips. *Thank you, Prince, yet again,* I muttered to myself. Freida grabbed a bucket of food and started running in pursuit of the runaway Prince. Colin unhitched the truck from the camper, simultaneously yelling at all the dogs to jump in the back of it, which of course those poor, bewildered creatures eagerly did. He then drove off to . . . he didn't know where! Meanwhile Freida tried to see which way Prince was heading and realized she couldn't see him anywhere. All she could hear were the sounds of screeching brakes and the blasting of car horns, and she imagined the worst; indeed we all did, blood and guts and bits of Prince splattered as far as the Acropolis. Prince by now had left the green grass and crossed the dual carriageway in central Athens, totally unaware of the mayhem he was causing. A kind lady offered Freida a lift in her car, and they stopped several bewildered passersby to ask if a large, ginger horse had passed that way. After about twenty minutes this generous lady was unable to help any further, and she dropped Freida off, she didn't know where. Then Freida received several offers of help

from men suggesting that she hop on the back of their motorbikes to continue the search for Prince. Freida took up one of the offers, the only one that she felt she was capable of getting her leg over the passenger's saddle without making a complete and utter fool of herself.

But this was not easy, with a bucket of food in one hand and a mobile phone in the other, whilst simultaneously trying to hang onto

a complete stranger for dear life. I mean if you are not a competent motorbike pillion passenger, where do you hang onto a complete stranger? In the meanwhile, Colin was phoning Freida and asking for her whereabouts. Just like a man, how on earth would she know! Freida tried to pinpoint her position by describing the advertising boards on the rooftops as they flew past. These really were desperate measures, if you know anything about Athens and the state of the rooftops. Just when Colin and Freida were beginning to think that they would never find each other, let alone Prince—well, not alive or uninjured in any way—there he was in front of their eyes.

He had managed to walk onto a building site. What had finally slowed Prince down was not exhaustion or even a desire to be found, but the newly laid concrete, which he was now wading through much to the annoyance of the driver who was currently sitting on the top of his huge concrete-levelling truck. He was not a happy man. But as I have mentioned to you before, Prince does not like to be caught, so he has to be approached ever so slowly and gently and quietly, preferably with a bucket of food in one hand. Only then by very slowly raising the other hand without him noticing it, and if you are ever so careful and gentle, he will allow you to take hold of his head collar. So Freida and Colin waded through the wet, sticky cement much to the amusement of the small crowd who have now gathered and to the even further annoyance of the man still attempting to lay the cement. But with the prospect of food, Prince allowed himself to be caught. Meanwhile, the news spread back to the stables, and several young men arrived to calmly walk Prince back to his bed. So that was the end of our trips out until we reached Crete.

Two days later we were off again, this time to catch the ferry from Patra to Souda on Crete. Unfortunately our driver was not as experienced as Jannie, and he parked our horse trailer close to the huge diesel trucks. It was the week before Easter, and the ferry was packed full of Cretan families all eager to return to their villages to join their extended families for the Easter festivities. Easter or Paska, as it is called, is a very big celebration, possibly the most important day in the Greek Orthodox calendar; we now realize. So instead of the fresh sea breezes that we had previously enjoyed, now we were subjected throughout the night to diesel fumes from the huge trucks parked all around us. Freida and Colin were concerned about us and asked the captain if they could go down below to check on us, but they were refused. Freida argued with the captain most of the night, but he was adamant in his refusal. Obviously he had no interest or concern for animals, and this should have been a bit of a clue as to what was to come in the future. Freida and Colin never gave it too much thought at the time and just put it down to a miserable and ignorant sea captain on the ferry. By the time we reached the Port of Souda, Prince was sick, very sick. He was refusing any food and even water.

But our new home was not far from Souda Bay, so the best thing was to get Prince out and into the field as soon as it was possible. We all arrived on 6 April 2002. It was a beautiful, hot April morning, and our first recollection was the sweet, intoxicating smell of the orange blossoms, which filled our nostrils like a perfume that only nature could concoct. Sadly, poor old Prince was totally exhausted, and he could barely walk out of the horse trailer. Colin raced down to the nearby river to get fresh water, not realizing that there was water connected to the field. Meanwhile Freida tied the five dogs to individual olive trees. They were unable to get directly onto the land, as there were drainage ditches all round it, so Prince and I were tethered under the shade of the neighbor's orange trees. I felt good, and I couldn't wait to get the turf under my feet and to enjoy a good roll on the soft earth. But Prince was too ill to move, and he was even refusing water. Freida took his temperature, and it was too high. Prince slumped; his head was down close to the ground. His legs spread apart, and it was all he could do to remain standing.

In true Cretan style, people passing on their way to their land stopped to say "welcome" to the raggle-taggle mob. We must have looked a strange sight so early in the morning, with an old camper, two horses, five huge dogs, and two rather distressed and weary English people. Freida met one local man introducing himself as the tax man, and her heart sank momentarily at the prospect of them meeting the tax man at a time like this, thinking to herself that surely the Cretans were not going to be so enthusiastic as to start assessing them for their taxes so soon! Another local man, whose family own a nearby building company, stopped to offer his help with Prince. He managed to explain that he had a horse, and so he kindly telephoned his vet and offered her services to Colin and Freida should they require them. This was a great comfort to have someone close at hand to help in this strange and new environment with such a sick animal to care for and without any knowledge of the language or where they could even find a vet. Meanwhile Colin had assembled the electric fence that they had brought with them so at least I could be turned out into the field to graze. Freida was rubbing Prince's gums with some medication in the hope of reducing his fever, and she continued to try to tempt him to eat and drink the cold mountain water that Colin had collected. For me, so much greenery without a connected electric fence was too much of a temptation, so I leapt it and headed off. I didn't know where to and cared even less. The feeling of the ground beneath my feet was tremendous after having spent one entire week standing all day in one position in a horse box. It had indeed been so exhausting, and now it felt so good to be free again. The opportunity to have a gallop was too good to be missed, but of course before I could get very far, Colin had jumped into the horse box, and it wasn't very long before he caught up with me.

Amidst much cursing and swearing, I was tethered to the rear of the vehicle and rather unceremoniously led back to where I had started and then tethered until the electric fence had been connected. Several hours later the old man—Prince, that is—started to show some signs of recovery initially by just sipping small amounts of water and eating one blade of grass at a time. Finally he was strong enough to walk the short distance into the field. Now four and half years later he is as fit as ever, and he and Colin make regular trips of two and a half kilometers to the beach in Kalives. But it was a scary moment at the time for all concerned, especially for Freida and Colin, who felt so responsible for their friend's condition.

With no farriers available on the island, Colin shoes and trims our feet. We have adjusted to the change in diet, and I now eat oranges, sweet ones only of course, and melon makes a pleasant change from apples and carrots. Polo mints are in very short supply these days, as they have to be imported from England. But we eat grapes in abundance, and they make an excellent substitute for polo mints. When we lived in England, Prince needed a very expensive medication for his chest complaint, which is called Chronic Obstructive Pulmonary Disease or C.O.P.D for short. This is a sort of emphysema in horses, which is generally caused by having been fed mouldy hay. (Poor old chap, he has had it rough. I really must try to make allowances for him; I keep telling myself.) However during the years that we have lived here in Crete, Prince has only ever had a couple of doses of the medication, which just goes to show you how much climate change can help. We seldom wear rugs either in the stable or outside. In fact we spend very little time in the stable at night except during the very cold nights and the wet months of January and February. Prince, on the other hand, is not too keen to be out of doors during the hot months of July and August, and so he spends most of the daytime hours inside during this time. Riding is much the same here as in England. Although there is not as much traffic; I am glad to say. We never hear a siren from an ambulance or those blessed fire engines. (They always used to unnerve me, even though I am bombproof.) We do find that walking on the other side of the road is rather strange, and this has taken time to adjust to. But the oddest thing that neither Prince nor myself can quite understand is the strange noises that the Cretan sheep make as they tiptoe along the lanes. It's a sort of ringing sound, not like a siren, nor like the church bells that we are so used to hearing on our Sunday rides to the pub in England. No, this is a dull clanging sort of sound. Anyway Prince and I are in full agreement on this matter, and we much prefer the prettier, quieter English sheep!

Three | Fate and Animal Protection

WE WERE COSILY ensconced in our rather "mature" four-berth camper on the land that had been purchased by us, solely because it was flat and green and classified as agricultural and therefore perfect for our two horses to graze on. Many of the plots of land that we had viewed were typical Cretan terrain, stony, terraced, and sadly lacking in grazing suitable for two large horses. We were delighted to have found our ten *stremma*, which were situated two kilometers away from the two nearest villages of Armenio and Neo Chorio. We had decided that we did not want to have any close neighbors, partly because we both enjoyed the piece and quiet of the countryside and also because we found it impossible to find a piece of land that was large enough to graze two horses, who theoretically require a minimum of three acres. Neither were we sure if having so many animals within the village limits would be acceptable to the local population. Our plot also supported one hundred small olive trees, which in time would grow, and we hoped they would give us and the animals plenty of shade.

Meanwhile, Colin had built a field shelter for the horses where they would be able to get some relief from the fierce Cretan sun during the hottest months of the year. Our five dogs were housed in their temporary home, which was a mesh compound with a roof, where they could be kept secure and dry. Even our precious ferrets had a home of their own made from bamboo, which we had hewn from our own land and built around one of the smaller olive trees close to the caravan. Finally Colin had managed to erect a waterproof shelter to protect our belongings and his tools, which we were expecting to arrive any day in a huge container.

We had purchased the land from two agents, who despite their words of reassurance, both now seemed to be conspicuous by their absence. We were finding their reluctance to contact us rather worrying as we had never received any confirmation from them that we actually owned the land we were now calling home. Eventually one of them arrived, and after a great deal of insistence on my behalf, he gave us the deeds to our land. In those early days we were totally trusting and naive to the ways of the Cretan businessman, and we had given the agent power of attorney in order for him to purchase the land at a good price on our behalf, or so he had told us. He had convinced us that he had legal representatives acting on our behalf, and his documentation showed that he was a member of the real estate governing body and other Greek authorities as well. So at the time we felt that we could trust him implicitly. How wrong we were, and in hindsight how very stupid we were as well.

But before we realized our dreadful mistake, we had also

agreed to have this man build us a house on our plot. It was to be a just a small, Cretan-styled house that would blend into the surrounding area, measuring seventy square meters in total living space inside but with a large verandah surrounding it where we could sit and enjoy the long summer evenings. George had told us, for that was the name of one of the agents, that he could build the house quickly and cheaply, so we paid him the first substantial amount of money to enable him to get started as we did not relish the idea of spending our first Cretan winter living in a camper. This sum of money included the cost of the planning permission and the money required to pay the builders' insurance known here as IKA. It was after paying this sum of money that we were visited by the previous owner of our land, a local man called Dimitri, who spoke very little English but seemed to be preoccupied with knowing how much we had paid for his property. To be quite honest, we found his preoccupation rather strange and just a little annoying as we had been told the price of the land by the agent, and he had assured us that the previous owner would not take less than the price that we had paid. Eventually Dimitri brought an English-speaking friend with him, and to our horror, we were to be told that the sum the previous owner had agreed on had very little to compare with what we had given to the agent. The crooked agent had indeed pocketed a vast sum of money whilst acting on our behalf, and the previous owner, who really as a Cretan man should have known better, had signed a blank document. There seemed to be very little that we could do about it, but it had left us with much less money than we had anticipated having to live on before we could find work. Little did we know that things were to get even worse!

The building work started, and we decided that we would just have to put it all down to experience and to move forward. After all, not only is it embarrassing to find out that you have allowed yourself to be conned, but neither did we want to be known as the whining and moaning English couple. Initially a team of Syrians arrived, and they worked very hard in the hot July sun building the concrete frame. Once they had completed their work and left, we sat and watched as one lone Albanian was sent to continue the rest of the build. Various other individuals came and went, but most of them seemed to do very little. It was painful to observe these so-called experienced craftsmen attempting to build our future and what was likely to be our final home, when it would appear that they had little or no knowledge about what they were doing and cared even less. There were times when Colin needed to show them how to do a variety of jobs and indeed to loan them the equipment with which to do it.

We were beginning to feel distinctly uncomfortable but tried to make allowances for a different way of building that was new to us, and indeed George was very reassuring every time that I spoke to him about our concerns. He always seemed to say everything that we wanted to hear, and now after living here for almost seven years, we realize that it is the Cretan way to always say what people want to hear, whether it be right or wrong, the truth or a downright lie; that is irrelevant in their mind-set. By now we had paid the agent a second amount of money, and he was demanding yet more. Things that we agreed on were not forthcoming; the roof was cracked and leaking like a sieve. The bathroom consisted of one white bath, which had been hastily positioned on a heap of rubble, and yet according to the contract, the bathroom should now be completed. It was time to consult with a lawyer, which we did, and we showed him the many photographs that we had taken of the awful workmanship. Once he had heard our story and seen the photographs, he had no hesitation in telling us to get rid of the builders together with the agent George.

Colin now enlisted the help of two young local Albanian brothers, and together they fixed the roof and tiled all the floors inside the house and the veranda. He hastily bought wood and made the windows and doors, fitted the kitchen, and plumbed in the bathroom—no mean feat when he had no electricity and no workshop to work in. I can vividly remember seeing him trying to work at his makeshift workbench in the garden with the chickens and cats jumping up onto his shoulders and among his materials. *Thank goodness I married a carpenter and a builder and not an office worker,* I frequently told myself, or the situation that we now found ourselves in could have been even worse. Once the basics were achieved, we moved into the house. Although we had no electricity, Colin managed to wire the house up to a small generator to which, during the hours of darkness, we were able to connect the television and fridge. Basic as it was, it felt good to be in a house again rather than to be living in the camper.

Our next challenge was to try to find the legal papers and to get copies of the planning permission, which after all we had paid for, and to trace the IKA payments, so we could get a permanent electricity supply, which in Crete you cannot have until those payments have been made. With no knowledge of the Greek language, and in those days very few friends to call upon, it really was an uphill struggle. Our next shock was not too far away after visiting the planning department, which incidentally had none of its information on computers, only in piles and piles of dilapidated and huge, outdated ledgers. I was soon to discover that the planning permission had never been applied for, as the architect responsible had not been paid for the limited work he had carried out. So now we realized that we were living in a house that had no planning permission and was therefore illegal.

These were certainly grey days for us. Our house was illegally built, and we had no work, no electricity, and no prospect of getting any either. Our surplus cash was disappearing rapidly, as we had paid for so many things twice, so we were watching every euro. Winter was now approaching fast, and we needed to find some work. Colin is an excellent carpenter, but even the best carpenter in the world needs materials and preferably a workshop or somewhere to do the work and to keep his tools. Of course ideally he also needs to have access to an electricity supply, but Colin had none of these, so he just had to make the best of it, which he did. I certainly needed to find some work, and therefore I franticly searched the ex-pats newspaper for a situation vacant. Eventually I found some work as a child minder in the evenings; it did not pay very much, but it was better than nothing. My vegetable patch was producing everything in abundance, and the chickens we had purchased were laying well, so we were never short of vegetables and eggs. Indeed, I even managed to sell my surplus eggs in the mini market in Kalives and my excess tomatoes to a local taverner.

There is a book shop in the nearby tourist town of Kalives called Papyrus, which is owned by an Austrian woman called Judith. After telling her that we needed to earn some money, she suggested that we consider starting a dog and cat hotel. She told me that many ex-pats had left the island as there appeared to be nowhere that their pets could be cared for when they wanted to go on holiday. It seemed like a very good idea. After all, we had the space, we both love all animals, and Colin could easily build the kennels that would be required. It would soon be our first

Christmas here on Crete, so we placed an advert in Judith's shop. We only received one phone call. Not a terribly enthusiastic response, we thought, but this one call gave us some hope. It was from a lady called Hilary, who had been caring for a deaf and blind rottweiler she had rescued. Hilary and her husband wanted to travel to England for Christmas, so they needed someone to visit the dog once or twice a day to check on her, feed her, and generally clean up after her. Terms were agreed, and we were off

Thankfully for us, Hilary had many contacts in the local real estate and building company, so she was also able to find Colin some carpentry work. Gradually the word spread, as Colin is an excellent carpenter and always fair and reliable, unlike many of the local tradesmen at that time, and demand for his work increased. In addition we were now getting more and more phone calls about the kennels and cattery.

Only one major problem stood in our way; we really did not have any spare cash with which to build the kennels. Thankfully my dear sister and my eldest son sent us some money, which was a lifeline and enabled Colin to build a small kennel block that would take up to six dogs. He worked long and hard searching for the cheapest fencing materials, and he made gates from some new pallets that he found. It is a wonderful experience to find and make things from nothing and so very satisfying, but as anyone who has done this knows, it is also hard work and so very time consuming. But now at least we had a real chance of earning some money.

On 15 December our first dogs and one cat arrived. The work seemed to go on forever, and we had very little time to enjoy our own Christmas, but we really did not mind as we were happy just to be earning a living again at long last. The last dog left on 10 January, but we had already taken some bookings for the following year. So now we felt like we really were in business. Eventually the word went around that people could safely leave their pets with us and that they were in experienced hands, so our business grew. Crete always seems to be drowning in bureaucracy, and therefore it is an uphill struggle to set up any business on a legal basis. When I initially consulted with an accountant, I was told not to bother to make the cat and dog hotel into a legal business as it would not be worth it. I suspect this advice was also based on the fact that so few Cretan people ever use a dog and cat hotel. Finally I managed to find an accountant who I could persuade that we wanted to work here legally, and so he set up a business for us based on Colin's carpentry and the dog and cat hotel, as well. Now we were really in business, and it was legal, and it gave us a small income that was enough to live on. We were able to save a little money as well, but the work was seven days a week and three hundred and sixty-five days a year.

We were managing to cope using our generator at night, although it could not heat the water. This meant cold washes in the washing machine, which in turn made me realize that we really do use too much electricity and heat too much water unnecessarily. The generator could not heat the iron either, and again I was amazed at how well we could manage without ironed clothes to wear, despite having enjoyed my Sunday evening sessions of ironing in the past. Now we were managing perfectly well without ironed clothes. The fridge could only work in the evenings with the power from the generator. During the summer months this was a little difficult but not impossible. It did mean that we couldn't keep much food in the freezer compartment, so we stored bottles of drinking water there, which meant that we always had a constant supply of ice-cold water to drink during the heat of the day. A solar panel on the roof ensured hot water when the sun was shining, but with no sun there was no hot water and therefore no shower unless, like my stoic daughter-in-law, you did not mind having a cold shower. During the winter months we resorted to heating a large pan of water on the wood-burning stove that Colin had installed. Thankfully it had an oven, so I was able to cook and bake cakes and biscuits in it as well as a rather splendid Christmas dinner.

There is no piped gas supply in Crete, so everyone uses Calor gas, and of course we had purchased an electric oven as gas ovens are less common and very expensive to buy here. In general I feel that we managed rather well. Of course during the summer months with the constant sunshine and, therefore, an abundance of hot water and light in the long evenings, it was easier to cope than throughout the winter months. During the winter months, all the work with the animals needed to be completed before it was dark. Living as we were, some distance from the village, there was no other form of alternative lighting to work by, so outside really was pitch black—wonderful for stargazing, but that was not a lot of help to us at that time.

When it was raining heavily, as it can do here, and the sky was grey, the house was dark during the daytime. It was miserable, and things felt bad. Also when you are feeling ill and need to get up during the night, struggling to light an oil lamp can be a difficult task; you feel very vulnerable. In general we are not the type to whine and moan, unlike some other people we have met, individuals who were so stressed because they had no electricity for a few days or they had been made to wait for this or that to be done. Telling them about our experiences and that we'd had no electricity for five years shocked some, surprised others, and some just couldn't give a dam, a question of "I'm all right, Jack."

I do not think that many people who we have met would have been prepared or able to have put up with our situation. But some ex-pats in those early days had equally horrifying experiences, like one family who had given their agent power of attorney to purchase a piece of land, and on arriving in Crete they found out that he had done just that, but that he now owned the land that he had purchased with their money. When we had discovered what a crook our two oh-so-friendly agents had been, I confronted one of their wives only to be told, "Well, you got a nice piece of land, and at the time we had some money problems," as if that made everything all right. When I contacted the various Greek authorities that George had led us to believe he was affiliated with, printing their logos on his business cards and his letterhead, I was merely told that he was not a member. Although I have to say that one of them did print a disclaimer to this fact in the local paper. Good, yes, but it did nothing to help us with our predicament.

Finally one day I was feeling rather low after having consulted with a local architect, who six months after telling me that he would sort out the problem for us, had clearly done nothing about it and had finally admitted that he could not do it. This meant that we had wasted another six months of telephone calls and visits to his office, endless hours of telling the same painful story over and over again. In desperation I decided to telephone Hilary, who was still working for the same local real estate agent in Kalives. I thought that maybe she just might know an architect who could help us. Hilary was indeed a great help, and she managed to get me an appointment and came with me to visit a reliable architect in Chania. After our initial appointment, he agreed to help us, which was no mean feat on his behalf, especially since here on Crete the architect is really responsible for the building. Should it be badly built and collapse or not be earthquake proof, then he is to be held liable. Obviously he required another vast sum of money to carry out the necessary work in order for us to acquire the planning permission for the house and for us to pay the IKA. Both of these government departments also requested that we pay a fine for not having done so in the first place. Then after five long years and a great deal of money, we celebrated with a huge party when our electricity poles were erected on our land. During those five years our business had increased, but we had both worked three hundred and sixty-five days a year and had never had a holiday together in all that time.

But somewhere in the great blue yonder, the spirits had heard me saying on many occasions in my life that one day I would dearly love to work with animals. They must have all had a really good laugh among themselves, and I suspect that they then agreed, "All right, let her, for now is the time." Like so many tourists to Crete during the preceding ten years, we had seen the occasional stray dog and lots of cats, but somehow the true extent of the problem had never dawned on us. After all, we were on holiday and wearing rose-colored glasses as most holiday makers do. During trips to the mountain areas, we had seen the occasional barrel dog, and we had given him some food and water. But we never really stopped to think that these poor creatures may spend their entire lives chained to tin barrels, which must be like an oven in the summer and like a fridge in the winter. We now know that they often have no food or water for days, no comfy warm blanket or bed to snuggle into, and too often an owner who may just kick him or her or beat them for the sheer hell of it. Bitches give birth frequently, and then the owner may well remove the pups at birth or soon after, not caring either for her loss or the physical pain that she may endure from the ensuing mastitis. When a bitch is chained to a barrel, she is also unable to take good care of her little family, as she would normally do. Young and inexperienced pups often stray onto the roadside and are frequently hit by passing cars or trucks, and there is nothing that their mother can do about it. For many of these poor creatures, their entire lives are sheer hell on earth.

In those early carefree days when we were living in our little camper, we had discovered two small puppies, which had been placed under our parked truck. We did not know what to do with them. But a German woman in the village of Armenio gave us the telephone number of another German woman who would possibly take them and re-home them in Germany for a small donation. So we had taken them to her premises in Chania, but even then we had still failed to grasp the full extent of the problem.

It was a few months after this incident that Colin and I spotted a huge brown-and-white hunting dog sitting in some long grass close by our home, and we naively assumed that he was with his owner. The following day we passed that way again and saw that he was still sitting where we had previously seen him. Only now the long grass that surrounded him appeared to be turning a yellowy brown colour. Obviously it had been sprayed with some form of pesticide or weed killer. The dog was drooling and foaming at the mouth, so we ventured nearer to see what the problem might be. This beautiful dog was very thin and very weak, and he had a cyst on one eye. He had obviously been eating the now contaminated grass, so together Colin and I carefully lifted him up and helped him as he struggled to walk the short distance to the truck. We drove him to our home, where he offered no resistance and appeared to be gentle and responsive. (Such characteristics can be found in almost all of the Cretan dogs for some unknown reason.) He soon settled into his new home, and we named him Mr. Dog.

By now we had discovered that there was an old council animal shelter that had been taken over by a German animal protection group called Arche Noah Kreta. This group had completely refurbished the neglected building. It now had puppy areas, isolation areas for sick animals, and an operating room. The vets were all from Germany and worked long hours in order to cope with their many charges. So we took Mr. Dog there, and the vet examined him, treated his eye problem, and vaccinated him, only asking us if we could keep him for a few weeks until he could be sent to Germany for re-homing. With regular food and care, Mr. Dog blossomed into a handsome Cretan hound. He was now strong and healthy, and his only fault was his incessant barking every night at five o'clock sharp until he was fed. Finally he was ready to go to Germany, and I felt pangs of guilt as we left him at the shelter, hoping that he would eventually find the family that he so deserved. This beautiful animal had obviously been abandoned by his owner.

I know now from vast and bitter experience that unwanted animals are often driven by their owners many kilometers away from their homes and the areas they are familiar with. Then they are abandoned by their heartless owners who do not care if they live or die, but for some reason the owners seem to feel secure in the knowledge that they did not end the animals' lives. It was purely an act of God. Of course the loyal dog just sits at the place that he was left and patiently waits for his owner's return. The reason for doing this . . . Well, there does not have to be any reason for animal cruelty or neglect here on Crete. Maybe a dog is getting too old to hunt or maybe he just doesn't come up to the owner's expectations anymore. If it is a female, maybe she has come into season or is pregnant or maybe the owner just does not want a dog anymore; these all seem to be reasons enough. Some owners who do not want an animal anymore, be it dog, cat, or even their loyal and once hardworking donkey, may take them somewhere, tether them to a tree, and leave them to die a slow and painful death from hunger and thirst, again safe in the knowledge that they did not directly end the animals' lives. It is a custom and a way of thinking that I really cannot even begin to understand, but for sure it must have been going on for generations here on this beautiful island of Crete.

One day when a young, intelligent, and articulate Cretan woman was visiting my place, she saw me treating a dog who had suffered third-degree burns at the hands of children. They had sprayed the poor animal with lighter fuel and then set him alight. She appeared just a little shocked, but her comment to me was, "What an awful thing for the children to do. After all, if you do not want a dog, then you just do not feed him." Another young woman, a teacher by profession, told me one day that her bitch had recently given birth to five puppies, but as she could not find homes for them and as they were now six weeks old, she was intending to take them to the mountains (where they would surely die)!

Suddenly now that our eyes were opened, we seemed to be finding so many dogs, like the emaciated and sick bitch that Colin caught sight of at the rubbish tip one bitterly cold winter's night. Her coat was the color of rust, and she was sleeping on a pile of rusty metal. She was unable to move very quickly, so he was able to catch hold of her, and he brought her home. She really did look so very close to death, and being inexperienced as we were back then, we were worried that she may have something contagious that she could pass onto our own dogs. So we made her a comfortable bed in the stable and gave her food and water. The following morning we took her to the animal shelter so she could be seen by the vets, who diagnosed pneumonia and called her Skinny Lizzie. Thankfully she recovered and was sent to Germany, where she was eventually re-homed with the organization Arche Noah Kreta.

It was on one of these visits to the animal shelter that I met a young and dedicated vet called Ines, who worked for the organization. Realizing that the shelter always seemed to be so full, I asked Ines if there was anything that I could do to help. Her response was quick, and she told me about five small puppies that had been discovered living in a nearby field. The vets were reluctant to take them into the animal shelter, as many of the dogs in there were sick, and there were many viruses that would surely kill these small puppies. So the workers had made a temporary shelter for them in the field, and they had been visiting and feeding them twice a day. Sadly now the Cretan owner of the field had told them all to leave, and he was threatening to poison the puppies if they were not removed that day. We had spare hotel rooms at that moment, so I agreed to have the puppies at our place. Ines brought them to me later that day, and I called them my "A-Team." They all were given names starting with the letter A, and so it all began. Within the week we had ten puppies, and we became a regular foster home for hundreds of small, abandoned puppies who could not possibly fend for themselves and who would have surely died without the care and attention that they needed and would normally have been receiving from their mother at their age.

Since that day, we have always had a place for motherless puppies. We have never been empty and are usually too full. Ideally we have space for twenty growing puppies, but currently we have more than forty ranging in age from three weeks to five months. We also have several older dogs as well as mothers and newborn pups. Thankfully we also have several dedicated volunteers who regularly take puppies, who have been found only hours after birth, into their homes. They can then bottle-feed them before returning them to us at around six weeks of age. It is a three-hundred-and-sixty-five-days-a-year job and with no financial rewards. Indeed we are constantly raising money in order to feed them all. It can be stressful at times, and the physical work can be exhausting, but the emotional rewards are priceless.

In recent years the German organization has left the shelter, much to the loss of the Cretan animals. But altogether I continue to work with three German organizations in a variety of ways, which I will explain in a later tale at the end of this book. We had not come to Crete to work with animals; indeed the thought had never crossed our minds. We were totally and blissfully unaware of the extent and the plight of the Cretan animals. Sometimes I wonder and ask myself what I would have done if I had known about the suffering of so many animals. Would we still have come here?

Was our ignorance an unconscious ignorance at that time in our lives? I believe in fate and that somewhere it had been decided that we would come here to Crete in order to alleviate some of the suffering of these poor, wretched animals. But I also believe that as human beings, once we become aware of our fate, then we are capable to a large degree of changing it and of redirecting it—our kismet—whatever name you choose to call it. But somehow I feel that my fate was sealed at that time. For whilst we can walk past a healthy, adult dog on the road, who is obviously used to being a stray, both Colin and I find it impossible to walk past a small, helpless puppy, who clearly will not survive if left alone. Neither can we turn away any sick or injured animal. Sometimes when I am feeling tired of the daily routine, I just wish that I could be like so many other people and turn my back on a helpless animal, but I cannot, and neither can Colin. We seem unable to stop what we are doing; perhaps the job satisfaction is too rewarding. Watching the tiny puppies growing day by day, seeing a sick or injured animal return to full health, encouraging a terrified and abused animal to come close by teaching it to trust again or maybe for the first time, this is all pure magic for both of us, and we have the gift of this wonderful magic every single day of our lives. *So why,* I ask myself, *would we possibly want to change it?*

Four | A Donkey's Tail

IT WAS JUNE 2002, and the day had started much the same as every other day since we had arrived on this beautiful, historic island of Crete. We were still living in our temporary home, the four-berth camper, with which we had traveled from England, camping on our plot of land with its one hundred small olive trees, waiting for the builders to start building our home. "*Sigar, sigar,* slowly, slowly," I could hear them saying. Indeed it was the first Greek word that I learned.

They were right, of course. As anyone who knows the Cretan way of life will tell you, nothing ever gets done quickly here. We had created quite an interest locally, living like a couple of nomads with our two horses, five dogs, one cat, and two ferrets. We had purchased two huge, white plastic pots for the purpose of washing our clothes. By the middle of the day, the hot Cretan sun would heat the water in the thick, black, plastic pipes, which carried our only supply of water, albeit agricultural water, to our plot of land. This meant that we had a regular and very cheap supply of boiling-hot water, provided that we were prepared to wait until midday for it. So, sitting on my three-legged stool by the open ditch, I could wash clothes in the way that generations of women had done so before the invention of the washing machine, and indeed in many countries they still do so today. It felt simple, basic, and thoroughly satisfying. But then it was only for the two of us. I am sure that I would not have felt quite so altruistic about it if I had been doing it for numerous children on a daily basis year in and year out and in all kinds of weather.

We usually got out of our small bed in the camper just before eight o'clock in the morning as the hot Cretan sun was beginning to invade our small, metal home. We were woken daily by the jinglejangle of the sheeps' bells as they were being led by the shepherd's little mongrel dog. I can assure you that no highly trained pedigree sheepdog could possibly be more obedient or better trained, more reliable, or more faithful than this little mutt. In hot pursuit was their shepherd Orthanos, who we had already named Bo Peep—cruel but true as his daily consumption of the lethal Cretan *raki* tended to make him drowsy in the hot afternoon sun as he sat patiently watching his sheep. On several occasions as the sun was going down, the sheep and the little dog, realizing that it was time to make their way back to the village, which was a distance of some two kilometers away, usually did so without his now sleeping master, frequently leaving Orthanos to wake up in the chill of the dark summer evening and in a panic as to the whereabouts of his lost flock.

In England we were used to seeing sheep grazing in a field surrounded by secure fencing of one type or another. Here on

Crete, the sheep are rarely if ever left unattended, except in mountainous regions, as there are virtually no fences to contain them. The shepherd tends to take his sheep to wherever they are able to graze. He does not necessarily own the piece of land, but he has possibly been allowed to graze his sheep there through word of mouth. Maybe the land is owned by a relative or a friend or even a friend of a friend, and he or she may not even live in the village. This piece of land may be in an olive or orange grove, and hungry sheep could soon strip the bark from the young trees, thus causing eventual disease and death if the sheep were allowed to wander where they chose. Of course there is always the additional problem here of stray dogs, who can so easily worry the sheep and even kill an entire flock if the sheep are left unattended.

"*Kalimera.* Good morning," Orthanos calls to us in Greek as he hurriedly tries to keep up with his flock, who are now gaining speed in their eagerness to reach their grazing after the long walk from the village. Where we are living, as I have previously mentioned, is rather isolated, and in those early days we rarely saw anyone walking past our place. So Orthanos was our first and only regular passerby, so to speak. He did not speak or understand any English, so it was just a matter of waving and lots of smiles in those days. But today was going to be a little different from any other day that we had experienced so far. Usually about half an hour after the sheep arrived at their grazing area, Orthanos would return to the village of Neo Chorio, and I suspect the local *kaffenion*, riding his small donkey, who had spent the previous night alone in the field. This old shepherd usually left his flock knowing that his loyal, little dog would not allow them to leave the open field. This charming little dog, who incidentally when I naively asked his name, was told that it was *Skilos,* which means *dog* in Greek. That should have given me another clue as to the general Cretan attitude toward their animals and dogs in particular in those early days.

Today on the return journey to his village, Orthanos was walking and carrying a small bag with bread in it, which was obviously intended for the donkey's breakfast, and a long piece of rope, which I recognized as the rope with which he tethered the donkey to the nearest clump of grass overnight. It is common practice here, unfortunately, when a donkey is not working that his/her front legs are tied loosely together (hobbled) to reduce the likelihood of him/her walking very far. Some forms of hobbling are worse than others, and some can be very cruel. If the hobble is made from thin rope or wire, then it can cut into the donkey's legs and restrict the circulation of blood, even causing a wound that can then become infected. (You will read later how even a small wound can become infected with the tetanus microbe and lead to certain death.) In some cases the poor animal's head is also tethered to his/her feet for hours on end to ensure that he/she is not able to eat the precious olive trees, a cruel and primitive practice that must have caused many a poor creature immense agony and misery under the hot Cretan sun.

As he walked past our plot of land, he talked to me (not realizing that my knowledge of the Greek language was limited to about half a dozen words at this stage). He looked worried, scratching his head in the same manner I had seen him do when searching for his sheep. Clearly his beloved donkey had not remained tethered overnight where he had left him, and the animal had decided to go walkabout and do his own thing. Perhaps I need to explain that the piece of land we had purchased is in a vast area of olive and orange groves on the western side of the island, and the olive and orange groves stretch for approximately thirty square kilometers. A huge river runs nearby, and our nearest neighbor is approximately two kilometers away. So you can appreciate the size of this shepherd's problem in searching for the lost donkey! Having no knowledge of the Greek language and having to rely on sign language, I tried to communicate to Orthanos that we would look out for his donkey and get a message to him should the animal be found.

Later that morning, as the temperature soared much higher than we English are used to, Colin and I decided to take our five dogs to the river. It was fast becoming a daily routine that also allowed us to regress from our fifties to those carefree days of our childhoods, wading in the icy cold mountain water and throwing sticks and imagining finding long lost treasure in the clear, running water. It was on the way back from our trip to the river that I spotted the donkey, a piece of the rope still trailing from one leg. He was happily grazing in the shade of an old olive tree, which offered the perfect protection for the creature on this hot June day. Colin took the truck and returned the dogs to our place whilst I waited with the donkey, readily equipped with a donkey-sized head collar, bread, and peppermints (as any equine lover will tell you are a must). I hardly dared to approach him, as my recent and only previous experience of a donkey had taught me that small as they may be they can bite and kick without any warning if they are so disposed. Tempted by the familiar smell of bread, he now came closer, and I managed to get the head collar on, although not fastened. Meanwhile, Colin had spotted Orthanos some distance away, and he went to get him. When the two men finally arrived and we all approached the little donkey in an attempt to catch him, that was when the fun really started!

Obviously enjoying his bid for freedom, this old boy was not going to give in easily, and he broke into a steady trot, weaving in and out of the olive trees, ensuring that we caught our clothing or bumped our heads at every turn on the long, low branches. He made his way up the steep hillside terraces, almost to the top, and when Orthanos managed to head him off and stop him going down the other side; he then went into a full gallop back down the terraces the way we had all come. We were now slipping and sliding and trying to hang onto the overhanging branches in an attempt to stop ourselves from falling head over heels down the rough hillside.

We all pursued this little donkey as he returned to where we had originally discovered him. But he wasn't going to stop now and give up his freedom that easily. Across the narrow, unmade road he dashed and on into a newly ploughed orange grove, managing to pluck the occasional fallen orange from the ground on the way. Juice propelled from his mouth as he munched the delicious fruit, highlighting for us all just how hot and thirsty we now were. The old shepherd was quick and nimble despite his years, but he was now sweating profusely, and my overactive imagination turned to the prospect of my having to give him cardiac massage on the Cretan hillside on this hot June day. Colin had given Orthanos a long piece of chain with which to hold the donkey once he was caught, and for one awful moment I thought that perhaps this old shepherd just might be inclined to beat the living daylights out of this Jack, when and if we ever did catch him, as a punishment for all the grief that he had caused us all. I considered that perhaps in hindsight a rope would have been better idea. Backward and forward we all ran, across ditches, through bushes and newly ploughed fields and freshly watered groves like three characters from an old black-and-white cops and robbers film. Finally, hopelessly cornered, the now tired donkey gave in, and his owner approached him, calmly put the chain through his head collar, and led him back to his resting place. Whatever he thought, I never heard a cross word from the old shepherd, who showed only gentleness and patience and an acceptance of this being just part of life and one of those things that happen from time to time. This is in much the same way, as I have since discovered, these Cretan people treat life and death and any of the events that fate throws at them.

Orthanos was obviously anxious at having left his flock unattended for so long, so I offered to ensure that his donkey was safe and secure, and I gave the now thirsty animal some water to drink whilst Colin drove the old man back to his waiting sheep.

With numerous thank-yous and offers of a beer in the local *kaffenion*, we all went our separate ways. It's maybe not so much a story as an event in some people's eyes, but it's an experience unique to us and one we would certainly not have had if we had remained in England.

Five—Ella's Tail

I WAS VISITING Kostas's place one day when he took me to look at an old, filthy, rabbit hutch, which was approximately three feet long by eighteen inches wide by twelve inches high. It was the usual sort of habitation for animals that I had become accustomed to seeing at Kostas's place, dilapidated and patched with an assortment of old pieces of plastic and mesh, all fastened together with well-used pieces of wire and cable.

But to my horror, inside was not a rabbit but a small one-time white, but now a filthy grey, urine- and feces-stained Bichon bitch. She was probably about one year old and not much bigger than the average rabbit. Kostas told me that she had belonged to a friend who lived in Athens. I now knew that meant she had probably once lived in a comfortable family apartment where she was no doubt spoiled and well cared for. But as was the case for so many families, the novelty had now worn off, and like an old toy, she was to be disposed of but without the family actually killing her themselves.

I know that in England and many other countries, a vet will put to sleep, or should I say euthanize, an animal just because the owner does not want it any longer. Here in Crete the vets will not do this, and whilst there are arguments both for and against this practice, they also refuse to euthanize kittens and puppies who are unable to fend for themselves. This in turn leads to many cruel and painful deaths for unwanted pets, such as being chained to a tree and then left to slowly starve to death. Dogs and cats are thrown from their owners' cars on the open road. Then often in a blind panic, they get hit by the first passing vehicle. Of course the owners can confidently convince themselves that it was not their hands that killed the animals. It was more an act of God or fate.

Kostas cannot speak or understand any English, but he is a good communicator, and he managed to convey to me that he had found another home for this dear little bitch. It was a home with a friend in the next village, but before he handed her over, he wondered if I could give her a bath. The poor animal appeared to be demented as she scratched and clawed at the wire and wood of her filthy, stinking, little prison. The tin floor was covered with the remains of the food he had given her, which consisted of bones and salad, obviously leftover food from the nearby taverner. She had no water, and her excrement covered the rusty metal base, which she was unable to avoid treading in. Willingly I agreed to take her and bathe her, and I quickly removed her from the cage. Once outside, the little creature jumped and ran around half crazed, obviously delighted to be out and able to move around in the long grass. Driving home with her was no mean task as she leapt about the car with excitement. Back at the camper, which was still serving as our temporary living quarters, I bathed her and shampooed her skinny little body. It was evident that she was not getting enough to eat. I offered her some food and water, which she eagerly consumed, and for the entire afternoon she lazed in the hot summer sun. I really hoped that Kostas would forget about her, but sadly, after a few hours he turned up and grabbed her by the scruff, handling her as if she were a rabbit or a chicken he was about to slaughter. He put her into his old, green, battered van and sped off with her. Hoping that she would soon be going to her new family and a better life, I tried not to think about it too much, as surely any family life would be better than the living hell she had been in.

In those early days here I really was quite shocked about the conditions in which I found these animals, and I hoped that what I was seeing was the exception. Sadly that has not been the case.

A few weeks later, I ventured to ask Kostas in my limited Greek what had become of the little white dog. To my total devastation he told me that he still had her and that she was still in her filthy little prison. "She needs a family," I kept trying to explain to him in limited Greek language and to a Cretan man with no knowledge of English. "She is not a dog who can live outside," I kept repeating in the hope that my message would penetrate.

But having seen Kostas in an angry and bad mood on a previous occasion when I prevented him from taking two small hunting dog pups I had found, I had no intention of falling out with him. Besides, we were still living in our small camper, and we really couldn't take on any more dogs at this time. Neither did I want to gain the reputation of being the mad English woman who takes away people's dogs. At that time we were still not aware of the extent of the stray animal problem. Nor did I have any thoughts or inclinations to find out about it or to care for those animals I had seen. Coming here from England, I somehow assumed that there would be organizations like the Royal Society for the Prevention of Cruelty to Animals around the next corner. For sure, I had not come to Crete to get involved in animal protection, and I honestly was not aware that there was such a huge problem.

We had been on holiday to Crete for five years prior to moving here, and yes, we had seen the odd stray dog roaming around, but all looked well fed and seemed happy enough walking along the beach. Oh, how naive and ignorant we were back then. Although now after only a few months of living in a Cretan village, I was beginning to form a slow and vague realization that there must be hundreds or even thousands of dogs all over Crete suffering as this little dog was. I felt totally impotent and did not know who I could ask for advice or help, thinking there was little if anything I could do. Still it hurt, and it was difficult to get this little dog's plight out of my mind. The thought of her scratching and scraping at her secure little prison and living in the filth and excrement without the basic requirements of food and water stayed with me like a torment that I tried to ignore, but the picture of her would creep back into my mind when I least expected it.

Now I rarely ventured to Kostas's place, as the sight of the little dog frantically trying to claw her way out of the hutch was becoming a recurring nightmare to me, nor did I want to be known as some interfering English woman who thinks that she knows better. We just wanted to blend into the village community and to keep a low profile. So it was perhaps about six months later, with so many problems of our own to deal with due to the corrupt builders we had unfortunately encountered, that I had finally succeeded in giving little or no thought to the suffering of the small prisoner, when one evening at the *kaffenion* Kostas asked me if I would collect the little dog again and shampoo her for him. Trying not to act too excited, I casually agreed.

Very early the next morning I was there, and I was surprised and relieved to find her not in her little hutch but tethered to a stake in the long grass. Instinctively she sat motionless and silent, obviously cautious of who the visitor was. She was so small that

I could so easily have run her over. Picking her up, I realized that her coat had now grown thick and matted like an old piece of grey, stinking felt. It was July, one of the hottest months of the year here in Crete, and she smelt foul. It was a cocktail of smells consisting of stale faeces, decaying rotten food, and urine, which had over the months stuck to her little body in layer upon layer. And with no chance of rainfall to wash it off, it had baked hard under the hot Cretan sun. The stench emanating from her small skinny body made me feel nauseous and revolted me, but nevertheless I hurried home with her lest Kostas should return and change his mind.

At home Doreen and Brian, who were friends we had met through Kostas, were waiting to say good-bye to us before they returned to England after their vacation. Doreen took one look at the little mite, and her eyes filled with tears at her sorry state. Three shampoos later, after wrapping the dog in a huge bath towel, I could now begin to cut her coat off, as it would have been quite impossible to groom her. Having only small nail scissors available, I made a start with her curled up on my knees. Her coat was not only felted, but it contained all sorts of insects and fleas and ticks, which bled profusely as I cut them with my scissors. Every conceivable type of grass and seed was trapped in her little fleece. It was just a question of lifting small sections of hair and cutting it as close to the skin as I could with the sharp pointed scissors. There were times when I unavoidably nicked her skin, but she never complained or even flinched with pain. Three and half hours later she emerged looking rather like a badly shorn sheep. But throughout the entire procedure, she had not struggled nor objected to anything that I did, and I suspect she had enjoyed the close human contact, which for sure she had not experienced in a very long time. I did not want to return this delightful little dog, who for some reason that I will never understand still had the spirit of an innocent and excited child as she leapt about the verandah. So I waited for Kostas to collect her. Days and weeks passed, and he didn't show up. I avoided him like the plague in case he asked me to return her.

Then one evening in the *kaffenion,* he told me that he had a friend that wanted to take her, and so he would be collecting her in a day or two. But again he failed to turn up, and yet still more days and weeks passed, until one hot sunny afternoon he arrived in his old green van, and my heart sank. The little dog was looking great, and surely he could not resist her. I felt sick with worry and wondered just where and to whom he was going to take this little white bundle of fluff. She must have been with us now for about two months. Her coat was clean and her curls were pure silk. She looked a picture of health and could surely be sold for a good price. She had already been in season, but it wouldn't be long before she would find herself pregnant, and who knows what would happen then? She could be turned out again and find herself on the street. I just didn't want to think about it. When she saw Kostas, she greeted him like a long lost friend and ran to his van as if to go home. *That is so typical of the loyalty of a dog,* I thought. *How could we humans abuse their trust so?* To my immense joy and delight, Kostas left without her; clearly he could see just how happy she was. Now I felt that perhaps, at long last, he had lost interest in her.

It was about one week later when Jan and Lenni, a Danish couple whom we had met the first week we had arrived here on Crete, turned up at our home. They were true animal lovers and always paid us a visit when they came here on holiday. As they sat on our verandah, they just couldn't leave the little dog alone and constantly played with her. I told them her sad tale, and they immediately asked me if they could take her back to Denmark with them. In those days I wasn't sure of the procedure, but she had already been vaccinated so it was just a question of checking it all out with the local vet in Souda. Danish laws are much more flexible than English ones, and Jan and Lenni spent the remaining days of their holiday sorting out the necessary paperwork and checking out the possibilities with their tour operator of getting the little white dog back to Denmark with them. They called her *Ella,* which in Greek means *come,* as it was about the only word that she ever responded to. So it seemed a very appropriate name for her.

Currently Ella still lives with Jan and Lenni, spending her weekends at their summer house. Her photographs show her living as if she were in heaven, sleeping in their bed and generally doing exactly whatever she pleases. Their other little dog, which was a very nervous Jack Russell before Ella arrived, seems to have also benefited, as little Ella's irrepressible spirit has rubbed off on him. He has gained in confidence and now follows her everywhere, giving him a new lease of life. Last year Jan and

Lenni drove to Crete to celebrate their twenty-fifth wedding anniversary and brought little Ella with them. She was a joy to behold, looking so happy and relaxed, so content, and still so full of life. Since then Lenni has met Kostas, and she has given him several photographs of Ella. When he received them, there was an expression of delight if not puzzlement on his face as he pondered over the photographs of her sprawled out on their bed and furniture. Little Ella's life has turned full circle now, the only difference being that her home is a secure one from where she will never be evicted.

Six | Nelson's Tail

IT WAS THE month of July in Crete, and as always it was very hot. The temperatures were in the region of thirty-nine degrees centigrade, an unbearable climate to be outside in for too long without water and adequate shade. There are no pools of rainwater for animals who are living on the streets to drink from. The last rain fell in the month of May, and no more is usually expected until late September or early October. The discarded food in the taverner bins is rotting and covered with enormous blue bottles. This waste food is now inedible except for the most desperate of stray animals. Many times newborn pups and kittens, who have been thrown into the bins whilst still alive, become live bait for these huge flies and blue bottles. I have rescued such babies, and after a few days I have needed to have them euthanized as the live maggots in their tiny bodies begin to emerge.

It was on such a day that Linda discovered a small white dog near the Port of Souda Bay. He was staggering along the road in the direction of the main highway. He was weak and close to total collapse and for sure a certain death should he have ever reached the busy street. He was skinny and lethargic, with a huge swollen belly indicating that he was suffering from intestinal worms and flea infestation. His gums were pale, almost white in color, suggesting anaemia and malnutrition.

Linda had spotted the poor little mite as she was driving home from work, and she had gathered him up just in time and brought him to me.

She carried him onto the verandah as he was too weak to walk unaided. His long skinny legs were shaking and unable to carry the weight of his body. His fragile frame was trembling with fear, but he was too weak to offer any resistance. This was not an attractive puppy by any stretch of the imagination. He was aged about three months, and he had coarse, short, white hair covering his entire body, and his face was covered with an array of light brown freckles. An umbilical hernia protruded from his already grossly extended belly, and I recall that my initial assessment was that he better resembled a pig than a puppy. Cradling him in my arms, I placed him in the isolation cage where he could rest far away from the other puppies for his own safety and just in case he was carrying any infectious disease that he could so easily pass to the other smaller and not-yet-vaccinated puppies.

Once settled on his soft clean bedding, the little puppy drank copious amounts of water but refused all offers of food, and then he quickly fell into a deep sleep. When Linda found him, he was barely able to put one foot in front of the other, and he was suffering from dehydration and exhaustion, so he continued to sleep for several days and needed to be woken up to be given food and water. After treating him for external and internal parasites, Nelson, as we had now decided to call him (the first naval-type name, albeit an English one, had come into my head ,bearing in mind that he was found near the famous Souda Naval Port), still showed no desire to eat either dog or human food. So I started to feed him miniscule amounts of a multivitamin cream, which takes no effort whatsoever on behalf of the recipient to eat and yet contains all the necessary vitamins and nourishment to sustain a small animal's life.

I frequently find dogs and puppies who are reluctant to eat dog food, despite their obvious hunger, and I suspect that this is because during their short lives they have never eaten or been offered it. These animals will usually eat only bread, which after all has probably been their staple diet since birth, and any food that they have managed to find would have been the remains of human food. Suffering as they usually are from chronic starvation, they have very little desire to eat, as their stomachs have shrunk over time. Over the past seven years I have given sanctuary to numerous starving dogs whose preference for food has been dry bread. It has often taken me several weeks to persuade them to eat dog food, and this has only been achieved by smearing small quantities of wet dog food onto their preferable diet of bread every day until eventually they accept it.

Nelson slept for three days and nights, and when I decided to take him to the house, he was still unable to climb the four small steps that led from the grassy area to the verandah surrounding our house. When he was introduced to the smaller pups in our care, whilst he made all the gestures of wanting to play, he usually fell over in the process of attempting to do so. Gradually he was well enough to join the other puppies in the puppy compound. Whilst Nelson was physically bigger and older than the majority of them, he remained a quiet and gentle dog who showed no signs of aggression toward his younger and weaker companions. Finally he was strong enough to be given the necessary vaccinations and to be prepared for his departure and eventual re-homing in Germany.

When the day arrived for him to travel with all the other dogs, a journey which at that time used to take three days over land, we took Nelson in a travel box to the place of departure, the old animal shelter being run by the organization Arche Noah Kreta. It was usual for us to stay with the dogs until they left and for me to make my tearful farewells, sure in the knowledge that they would eventually be found a home. But on this occasion we had other urgent business, so we were forced to leave Nelson outside the shelter sitting in his box. Seeing the look of total disbelief and abandonment on his face as we walked away was so upsetting, that look in his eyes stayed with me for a long time. He must have thought that we had betrayed him and left him alone and unable to escape from his little prison. Nelson was not a cute puppy by any stretch of the imagination, and yet I desperately hoped that someone would give him a loving home. Surely his gentle and kind nature would shine through his awkward and unattractive outward appearance?

The following Christmas Ines the vet returned to Crete from Germany in order to help out at the animal shelter. As usual she came to visit us, and this Christmas she handed me an envelope, which she thought I may like to have. When I opened the envelope, inside there was a photograph of the most beautiful, enormous, white dog with orange freckles on his face, just like in the fairy story written by Hans Christian Andersen about the ugly duckling who grew into a beautiful white swan. Nelson had been transformed from an ugly puppy into a very handsome white dog. Now he looked happy and confident, and the photograph showed him lounging on a sumptuous red bed by an open fireside. There was also a letter from his new owners thanking for me for this wonderful dog. What a unique and priceless Christmas present, possibly the best one I had ever received, and I cried tears of joy and happiness and satisfaction. I replied to

Nelson's new family, who had liked the name I had given him so much that they had decided to keep it. By return post, I sent them the details of the circumstances in which Nelson had been found, and I enclosed the photographs of the skinny, ugly, and starving little dog who had been delivered to my door. They in turn replied to me and admitted to feeling so shocked by the photographs that they had both been unable to stop crying from what they had seen and read. Realizing for the first time just how much their beloved pet must have suffered, they also told me that the information had helped them to understand why Nelson still had a constant need for food and love. Although clearly from the photographs that they had sent to me, he now had an abundance of both. So this small, skinny, ugly puppy who no one had wanted and who had been abandoned to face an inevitable, slow, and agonizing death by accident, starvation, and thirst, now lives with a family where he is warm and well fed and where he obviously has a never-ending supply of love and kindness. What dog could ask for more?

Seven | Christmas Tails

WHAT IS IT, I ask myself, *about the human condition and Christmas and animals?* Half of the population here on Crete appear to want to own a puppy, even if it is only for Christmas, and the other half seem to want to dump them, usually on me!

Christmas 2005. It is Christmas Eve, and the weather is wet and cold here in Crete, the sort of cold that seems to penetrate through to your bone marrow, icy and sharp and at times painful. It is probably the same in England, but maybe it appears to be colder here because the daytime temperatures can be quite pleasant at this time of the year, or maybe it is because the high water table in this area where we are living lowers the temperature at nighttime.

To the local Cretan village people, this area is known as *Limni,* which means *lake,* and they would never choose to live in this area as they are convinced that it is too wet and therefore teeming with mosquitoes. But this year it has been raining for the past two days and nights. Working outside with the animals means several changes of clothes, and with no electricity the house seems dark and dismal. I try to remind myself that this is how people have worked and coped for generations. It is a fact that in the village of Armenio, no one had electricity until the 1960s. We don't have a lot of money either, and so we are rather frugal about using the generator as it guzzles the diesel. Everywhere is wet, muddy, grey, dirty, and so very cold.

Colin is in his usual hurry to get to the local *kaffenion* for his pint of beer and a few glasses of the local brew known as *raki*. I feel that he has to be reminded as he leaves the house that perhaps it would be advisable to collect the turkey from Kostas the butcher first, bring it home, and then return for the evening's merriment rather than risk our Christmas dinner being left hooked casually on the back of the old wooden *kaffenion* chair all evening and even possibly forgotten altogether. Ten minutes after Colin has departed, he returns with a large, dirty, and foul-smelling plastic sack in his hand. The aroma arising from it hits the warmth of the room and reminds me of raw fish and river water. I am just hoping that our turkey is not in the bag. Surely Kostas the butcher would not do such a thing. His premises

are immaculate. Wearing his long white apron, knee-high, white, rubber boots, and tight, short shorts, with his Cretan olive skin and jet–black, receding, curly hair, he cuts quite a dashing figure strutting about the plateau.

When we initially settled here, it was not very long before we were invited to go for a beer at the local *kaffenion* in Armenio. It was immediately apparent to me that Kostas and his butcher shop were as much an integral part of the community and social rendezvous as the *kaffenion* itself. Situated on the opposite side of the road to the *kaffenion,* it is only a few paces away from the tables and chairs placed underneath the ancient eucalyptus tree, so typical of *kaffenions* all over Crete, where the local village menfolk have gathered together for generations to play backgammon, to partake of the local fruits of the vine, to discuss the village politics, or just to while away the hours discussing their vegetables, sheep, goats, and the politics of farming. Where Kostas's shop is situated, with its excellent quality of meat, fish, vegetables, and his delicious varieties of cheeses, one can so easily purchase the entire family's requirements whilst simultaneously drinking a glass of wine.

Indeed it is quite usual for Kostas to offer a glass of his excellent local *raki* whilst you are waiting to be served. As a woman, I tend to feel just a little self-conscious entering this largely male-dominated establishment, as the majority of the customers do appear to be men. Kostas's opening hours appear to equate equally well to the opening hours of the *kaffenion,* as in the early mornings a local Albanian woman cleans and serves

until Kostas arrives. This can be anytime after 10:00 a.m., but it is not unusual to find him still working hard preparing fish or making one of his delicious cheeses until three or four in the morning. Throughout the evenings, he can be seen wandering across the plateau from his shop to the *kaffenion* and back again as the customers come and go. On the very rare occasion that Kostas is away, it is not unusual for Mixali, the proprietor of the *kaffenion*, to have access to the shop and to serve the occasional impatient customer, despite his all-too-apparent lack of experience in cutting the meat. But no one seems to mind, as he is frequently aided and encouraged by any number of people who may be passing by at the time. It is also quite usual for waiting customers to take charge of the till, giving and taking cash to enable Kostas to continue his butchery skills without interruption. I feel sure that this would never happen in England, to allow one's customers a free reign of the premises, but in this small and close-knit community, everyone is known, and in the main everyone is trusted. In addition the Cretan attitude and distinct lack of health and safety rules is what makes life here so simple and refreshing.

Colin now stumbles through the lounge doorway and puts the heaving sack on the tiled floor in front of the open log fire. As he does this, brown, stinking water oozes out of the plastic fabric. I peer inside, and I can see the four small heads of four little puppies, who are all shaking and shivering from the cold and fear. They are soaking wet and look as if you could squeeze water from their small furry bodies. They are icy cold to the touch, and I consider that they must have been in the cold and the wet for hours judging by their condition.

Grabbing towels, we rub their little bodies; trying to dry four of them with two pairs of hands is difficult. All seem in such a desperate condition, as they are weak now and in need of immediate help. We are trying to not only dry them but to increase their circulation and stop them from shivering. They are no more than six weeks old and obviously terrified, allowing us to do whatever we choose to them. They are so vulnerable, and you could not help but wonder how anyone could abuse such weak and fragile beings.

Having spent twenty-two years in social work and the majority of that time dealing with abused children, I have witnessed the same sort of behavior in small children as I now see in puppies and other abused and vulnerable animals. And I wonder how we humans, with so much ability and power, can be so cruel to creatures who need our help and respect. Pulling out a drawer from under our bed, we empty its contents and fill it with blankets, towels, and hot-water bottles, and then very slowly, their fragile little bodies begin to feel a few degrees warmer. I name them Gold, Myrrh, Frankincense, and Star. Quite apt, I feel, for Christmas Eve, and they spend their entire first Christmas sleeping and eating in front of our huge, open log fire. They hardly make a sound and hide themselves from our view as much as they are able. Gradually over the Christmas period they start to gain a little confidence and eventually they are strong enough to be introduced to our other small resident puppies, where they eventually develop into confident and sociable little dogs.

Gold and Myrrh were sent to Germany and easily found good homes. Franky and Star were adopted by an English couple living here on Crete, and so I see them on a regular basis when they visit my dog and cat hotel.

Christmas 2006. Christmas cards start to arrive for us at the local *kaffenion*, as we do not have the luxury of having a post person here. One of the Christmas cards contains photographs of Franky and Star in their new home. Receiving photographs of the animals whom we have cared for raises our spirits in a way that cannot be described. Animal protection is hard work both physically and emotionally, and at times you feel drained and wonder just how much longer you can continue doing the work. Photographs of my little charges now looking so happy and secure help me to cope with the work during those dark dreary evenings when it feels like I am the only person working outside and would rather be in front of a large open fire watching the television or reading a good book.

But today is 19 December; it is just one week before Christmas day, and the cat and dog hotel is full and overflowing with last-minute requests from ex-pats who want me to take care of their dogs and cats after obtaining cheap flights to England for the Christmas holidays. Thankfully in Crete, Christmas is still, in the main, a religious celebration about the birth of Christ, and therefore life goes on in much the same way as any other day except for the additional church services, which suits me fine.

I receive a phone call from an American woman living in nearby Kalives, telling me that some local boys have found a puppy sitting in a disused drainpipe. The puppy is very cold and dirty and aged about five or six weeks, with what should be a pure-white fluffy coat and a jet-black head. The woman is feeling desperate as she is just about to depart for her Christmas holiday in Athens. Thankfully she agrees to bring him to me, but she has bathed him, which she obviously thought was the right thing to do. But this means that I cannot use the parasitic fleas spray now for several days. "Never mind," I tell her. "You will know better next time," and she leaves him with me. I call him Panda and welcome him into the fold.

On 20 December after spending time caring for Panda, the week's work is getting a little bit behind. So now I am rushing to the shops in between doing all the cleaning and feeding. I need to make sure that I have enough food in stock to feed the forty strays and twelve hotel dogs and twelve hotel cats over the Christmas holidays. The local village shop doesn't stock the sort of things that I need for the animals, although the two young women who have grown up in Germany and run a small mini market in Kalives have been very helpful and supplying me with the quantities of animal food and other items. First I go to the bank and then on to the post office, where I have to search through a box that contains everyone's letters in an attempt to find mine. The post is not in alphabetical order or even date order, so it is just a matter of sifting through the entire contents to see if I have anything there. Three little slips of paper tell me that we have three parcels, so then it's a question of lining up at the desk to get them.

Just as I am about to leave to return home, I receive a phone call from our friend Hilary, who is still working in a local real estate office in Kalives. Hilary has proven herself to be a true animal lover and protector after she rescued six puppies aged around five weeks from a mountainside. She had been travelling in her car along a lonely mountain road when it ground to a halt after running out of petrol. Hilary then attempted to telephone her husband only to discover that her mobile phone had run out of credit. Her only alternative was to walk a considerable distance to find the nearest telephone box, and whilst doing so Hilary heard the pitiful cries of several tiny puppies. Following the sounds, they led her to a steep incline, where she saw an old cardboard box. She quickly realized that the puppy cries were emanating from within the box. There was no doubt that someone had tried to dispose of the puppies by securing them in the box and then hurling the box down the steep mountainside. Without considering her own safety and the fact that no one knew where she was, and without a mobile phone that she was able to use, Hilary scrambled down the crumbling mountainside to retrieve the heaving box, which she was soon to discover held no less than six small girl puppies aged at about six weeks of age. Obviously the puppies' owner had thought that his crime would not be discovered in such an isolated place and that no one could possibly hear the puppies' desperate cries for freedom. But Hilary had struggled unaided and saved them all, and what is more astounding is that she has kept them all, as she was unable to make the heartbreaking decision of which ones to part with.

Hilary tells me that an English couple who were hoping to spend Christmas in their Cretan home have arrived at the office holding a small, grey, fluffy bundle with the face and features of a friendly owl, but she seems unable to walk and is in obvious pain. I quickly leap into the truck and drive to the office where Hilary is waiting with the English couple and the puppy. The puppy is a girl, and she is about four weeks old at the most, whimpering and in constant pain. The couple tell me that they found her lying on a quiet road near their home. It is quite possible that she had been thrown out of a moving vehicle, and I suspect that she may have either a broken leg or pelvis. One quick telephone call to George the vet in Souda, and despite the fact that he is trying to get away for a much-needed Christmas break with his wife, he agrees that I can take the little puppy to his clinic. Angel, as I have now named her, is X-rayed, and George confirms that she has indeed suffered a fractured pelvis. She will need to be kept in a small box, so she is unable to move about for at least one month to allow for the healing process to take place.

In casual conversation whilst George is examining Angel, he happens to mention that a local Cretan lady had arrived at his clinic earlier that morning and told him that she had seen five young puppies abandoned in the nearby cemetery. George had advised her to ensure that they had food and water, as there was little else that could be done. With no animal shelter that can be used and no interest from the local Cretan community or local council to have one, there is not a lot that anyone can do other than what we are trying to do, and that is to assume responsibility as an individual. Having been given this information, I know that I have to go and at least take a look despite George's requests for me to resist, as he knows just how full my place always is.

"How can I rest over Christmas," I tell him, "knowing that they are there without food and water and warmth?" George feels guilty now for telling me about the puppies, but we have a firm and good relationship, and he understands that I have to at least take a look, so he agrees to wait whilst I do so.

The cemetery is only two minutes away from his surgery by car, but it covers a vast area of land and has several entrances. I park the truck at the nearest gateway and walk in, but to my dismay there is not a living soul in the place. I start to walk along the neat gravel pathways, searching for the abandoned puppies. *It is going to be like looking for a needle in a haystack,* I tell myself, because puppies who are afraid and alone instinctively know to keep quiet and hidden from view. The chance of hearing or seeing them is very unlikely. I realize that I will have to start searching the numerous bushes and shrubs that are growing everywhere, and so now I feel rather downhearted as I look around me at the vast area I need to explore. Realizing it would take a team of people hours of hard work to find these puppies, I wonder what chance I have alone. Knowing that George is waiting back at the clinic and trying to get away for his holiday, I feel that time is rapidly running out. I am also conscious of how long I have been away from home after having told Colin that I was popping to the shops for half an hour, and that was about two hours ago. I am already going to arrive home with an injured pup that will be spending Christmas in the house with us. I reassure myself that at least Colin is the sort of man who would be doing exactly the same thing if he were in my shoes. In addition, just as I was leaving the clinic, George's entire family had arrived there and were obviously anticipating leaving with him. That was almost half an hour ago. The puppies were not going to give themselves away; that I could be sure of.

It is at times like this that I have no hesitation on calling on Mum and Dad and any other departed soul that would like to help me. So I asked if there was anyone there who would kindly assist me in some small way and point me in the right direction where I could find the pups. No sooner had I finished my request then a young Greek woman appeared from nowhere and walked toward me. I assumed that she had come in through the nearby gate, although I had not seen or even heard her arrive. She walked toward me and stood by the grave that was nearest to me, and then she crossed herself. We exchanged smiles, and I apologized for my limited knowledge of the Greek language, asking her if she had seen any puppies in the cemetery on her recent visits. Thankfully this lady spoke perfect English, and she immediately pointed to the furthermost corner of the cemetery and took me to where the puppies were hiding! The puppies had split up, so two of them were sitting huddled together for warmth and comfort on a marble slab, well hidden from view by a huge overgrown shrub. The remaining three were sitting some distance from them in the shelter of the old stone wall that was covered in dense climbing plants. When they saw us, they instinctively turned their heads away in an attempt not to be seen and to show nonconfrontational signals. I would never have found them without this lady and the help of the dear departed souls. I thanked her and them as she eagerly assisted me in gathering up the puppies and putting them on the backseat of the truck.

Quickly now I drive back to the clinic where George's family rushes outside to greet me; they enthusiastically gather up the pups to show him. George gives them all a brief examination before I set off for home with six new arrivals for Christmas, a great deal later than I expected but with a lighter heart than I would have had if I had not gone to look for them. When I arrived home, I explained to Colin about what had happened and how after just intending to pop out to the shops, I had managed to come home with six puppies. He accepts the situation as I knew that he would but mutters as he feels that he has to, "Now that is it. No more puppies until after Christmas." And I wholeheartedly agree with him, but then . . .

It is Sunday, 25 December, four o'clock in the morning, and I am woken up by the cacophony of forty-four stray dogs and puppies and twelve hotel guests. Even Leo, our recently rescued purebred Belgium Shepherd, who is currently fastened up at the back of the house, is also barking. I lay there for a moment trying to assess the sort of barking it is. For example, there is the "we have spotted a cat" bark, or the "playful" bark or the "pack attack" bark, but that is unusual in the night and generally kept for feeding time or when a new arrival is introduced into the group/pack. No I decide this is more like a "there is a strange dog here" sort of bark. Certainly from time to time, a stray may venture close to the house. If there are any stray dogs in the vicinity, they tend to lay low during the day and come out at night, but I have never known any of them to enter our garden, especially during the hours of darkness. When you don't have electricity and there are no streetlights outside, everywhere is pitch black. When you are reliant on a torch battery and a small bedside lamp, which is also battery operated, then believe me; you do not leap out of bed as you might otherwise have done if it were just a question of flicking a switch to get a light on the situation.

Leo doesn't usually join in the barking contests with the other dogs, as he is so far away from them. So I wake up Colin, who is rather hard of hearing at the best of times and even worse after a few beers and *raki* at the local *kaffenion*. Certainly his hearing loss does preclude him from a great deal of additional stress where the dogs are concerned. There are times when it does appear to be quite an advantage, for example when you are running a dog and cat hotel and someone's beloved pet insists on barking and howling all night in the desperate hope that he or she will be taken home to their nice comfy bed. Could it be that one of the dogs has gotten out and is running free and upsetting everyone? Sure enough, I can hear the voice of a small dog coming from the area behind the house; all the dogs that we keep are at the front of the house, so they can be seen easily by us at every opportunity. If one should ever escape, they always come to the verandah and scrape at the door to be let in. No stray animal has ever run away from here. I am beginning to fear the worst as I do not recognize the bark that I am hearing, and believe it or not, like a mother knows her children's cries, I do know the barks of all my dogs and puppies and even the regular guests in the hotel. So now I am suspicious that someone has dumped a dog or puppy at the back of the house. It is 4:15 a.m., and it is very dark and extremely cold both inside and outside our small house. I grab a huge torch, which we have learned to keep in the same place to avoid falling about the room whilst looking for it often— I have to admit—amid much cursing and swearing.

Colin as usual shows no sign of leaping out of bed to investigate. I often wonder what it would take for him to say, "No, my dear, you just stay where you are in the warm, and I will take a look," like they do in the films. *Oh well, it is no use dreaming,* I tell myself. I venture outside in my slippers and dressing gown to investigate the situation, taking with me my not-so-brave house German shepherd for comfort. There I can plainly see, tied to a metal post in the road opposite the driveway to our house, not one but two medium-sized dogs. They have rope nooses tied tightly round their necks and securely fastened to the post, which means that the more the dogs attempt to pull free, the tighter the rope becomes. They were clearly not intended to escape. I return to the house to get a knife, as it is the only way to release the rope that is now slowly choking them both. Once released, they leap up at me, and of course they show no signs of running away. But I have nowhere to put them, as everywhere is full to capacity.

Naively I ask Colin what he thinks I should do; don't ask me why! At times of stress, we woman do stupid things like asking a husband's advice. He is annoyed that anyone should be so callous and selfish and suggests that I cut the dogs loose and let them go. I try to tell him that they are already loose and show no signs of going anywhere. I am frustrated but more annoyed at the heartless and thoughtlessness of the dogs' owners. What would two small and obviously very young dogs do anyway if they did leave? They would probably get lost in the hundreds of kilometers of orange and olive groves that surround our place and eventually end up tied to a barrel on a freezing mountainside or shot. Even worse, they could be poisoned and probably die a slow and painful death. So reluctantly I take them to the verandah, and with a collar and lead, I secure the largest one to the wooden bench, knowing that the smaller one will not leave her. As I am doing so, my torch light catches a glimpse of a brightly colored bag, and I go to investigate. It is a small bag of Chappie animal food propped up against the fence post, and with it are the dogs' vaccination papers oh-so-carefully wrapped in a plastic bag. *Not the work of a Cretan person,* I tell myself. *This is undoubtedly the action of an English ex-pat.* They have tried to erase the dogs' names, their address and telephone number, and also the vet's details, but I recognize George's handwriting, so I know that he will know who the owners are. But of course he is now closed for Christmas, and although I know that if I had an emergency he would be there for me, he also knows that I would not abuse his dedication over something like this.

Having settled the dogs down, I go back to bed, but of course I am wide awake now and unable to sleep, unlike Colin, who is snoring soundly beside me. As everyone who has any sort of sleep dysfunction knows, any problem appears to be so much worse in the middle of the night. All those little anxieties that pass your mind in daylight hours and are quickly dealt with and evicted seem to become monstrous, insurmountable problems, real dilemmas during the nighttime hours. What about the cat with no eyes, who sleeps on the verandah? Will they kill him? What about the week-old lamb in the field? What about the sheep? Maybe they are sheep chasers. I am unable to cope with all these anxieties and thoughts rushing about uncontrolled in my brain.

So I get up again and rummage through the draw on the verandah for another collar and chains with which to secure both the dogs to the wooden bench. Then I check on Thoskos, the cat with no eyes, and find that he is fast asleep in his usual place. Next I make sure that the sheep look undisturbed, and for the second time I get back into bed and try to sleep, knowing that in a few hours' time, I have a lot of work to do. All the dogs are still barking, chaos still reigns supreme outside, and I can tell that everyone is unsettled by the night's events and the two strangers who they all know are now on the verandah. Sleep evades me, and I get up and make myself a cup of coffee. I light the various oil lamps that we have scattered about the place, then I clean up Angel and feed her and console myself that I have completed one of my first tasks of the day. By now it is 5.30 a.m., and it is still dark outside, so I sit myself down at the kitchen table and attempt the *Daily Mail* bumper Christmas crossword puzzle. *Merry Christmas*, I tell myself, and wait for the dawn to break on what will most certainly prove to be yet another very busy Christmas Day.

Christmas 2007. It is one week before Christmas, and as always the hotel is as full as ever over the holiday period, as luckily for us and our kennel and cattery business, many ex-pats just cannot resist an English Christmas, with all the hype and all the usual hustle and bustle, not to mention the dreadful expense. I still much prefer the quieter local Christmas. Thank goodness where animals are concerned, one day is very much like another to them and us. This year yet again in the week preceding Christmas, it is raining profusely, and today I am really loath to start the morning's work, hoping that if I stay in bed just a few minutes more the rain may stop.

It is 9 a.m., and I am not yet dressed when my phone starts to ring. On the other end, there is a frantic voice asking me for help. It is Judith, the Austrian woman who owns the local bookstore called Papyrus in Kalives. She sounds very upset and rather panicky and tells me that she has just witnessed a small white dog being run over, not only by one but by three cars one after the other, and yes, not one of them had stopped. She tells me that the little dog is laying in the road, and she is standing over him, but she does not know what she should do. I suggest that she move him as carefully as she can to a safe place, preferably onto a firm surface, that she cover him with a warm blanket or coat, as he is sure to be suffering from shock, and that she remain with him until I arrive. I dress quickly, grab my mobile phone and a warm blanket, and drive to where they are waiting. The little dog is still alive, but by checking his gums, I can see that they are very pale, and he is certainly in shock. He is laying on a stiff doormat, so fortunately this makes it very easy to lift him onto the backseat of the truck, and I cover him with my warm blanket. The little dog was laid outside the bicycle shop, which is owned by a local Cretan man who is very worried about his doormat. So I have to assure him that it will be returned as soon as possible. *What a time,* I tell myself, *to be worried about an old doormat!* I telephone my wonderful vet George just to let him know that I am on the way with the little dog to his clinic in Souda.

Once in the clinic, I start to remove the blanket, and I am amazed that there are no obvious signs of injury. The little chap is looking around, although he makes no attempts to get up. But he could have internal injuries, so I leave him with Nicol the English veterinary nurse (the only one that I know of on Crete as English veterinary nurse qualifications are not accepted here and there is no such thing as a Greek veterinary nurse on Crete.) Then I head for home, knowing that it is still pouring down with rain, and now I am about two hours behind with the morning's work. When I telephone George later in the day, he tells me that the little dog is stable, and to everyone's surprise and delight, he has no broken bones; he is merely bruised and sore, but otherwise he seems fine. I call him Santa, and I take him home where he spends the following week resting in a box in our house. One week after Christmas, Santa is fit and well enough to join the other puppies, where he is lively and noisier than most of them. Thankfully Santa continues to make good progress and is quickly re-homed in Germany.

A few weeks prior to this episode, when I had been doing one of my brief visits to the shops in Kalives (for me, shopping trips are always brief as I can never afford the luxury of window shopping), as I drove past the local cemetery, a skinny black pup raced out from the entrance and chased my car. I glanced through my near-side driver's mirror, and I could see that he was determined to catch up with me. His long skinny legs made him look like a small racehorse on Derby day, and I could not resist slowing down for him. As I did so, he reached my driver's door and stood and looked at me as if he was expecting to see some-one that he knew. I opened the door and looked around to see if there was anyone out there who might know who he was. (Stupid thoughts, really, as there never is anyone . . . Somehow I still half expect someone to admit that this is their puppy who has escaped, and they are grateful that I have found him. See, I still believe in make-believe and happy endings.) Well, back to reality . . . No one was going to pick up this little chap if I didn't. *But how did he know to chase my car,* I asked myself? He allowed me to pick him up and place him gently in the back of my old Volvo. Once inside, he quickly found a box of books that I was storing for the next garage sale, and without any hesitation, the little pup climbed on top of the books and went to sleep. I continued with my shopping trip and returned home.

Peter, for that was now his name, was placed in the isolation pen, just in case he had anything nasty that he might pass to the other pups. The pen is close to the house, and there I could observe him for a few days to make sure that he was eating and drinking and going to the toilet okay, whilst at the same time, I could treat him for intestinal worms and external parasites, such as fleas and ticks, which he was sure to host. This has always been my procedure when accepting new arrivals. About week later, Peter seemed to be all right, although he had indeed been heavily infested with roundworms. He had been eating well, and so I made an appointment for him to have his first vaccination. On the day that I was due to take Peter and some other puppies for their vaccinations, I went to his pen, and as I reached out to pick him up, he laid down on the floor. What I at first thought was a game I then quickly realized was an epileptic seizure. It appeared to be short–lived, so I placed him in the car on the passenger seat and set off for our appointment with George the vet. Obviously he could not now be vaccinated after experiencing a seizure, but at least George could check him over for me. On our arrival at the veterinary clinic, Peter seemed fine although hyperactive, otherwise he was much his old self. George examined him and he took some blood to test in an attempt to see what was going on with this little dog's body chemistry. Peter then became fractious, but when I stroked his temples, he totally relaxed as if in a trance, and eventually he fell asleep. On our return to the house, Peter seemed to be all right, and with a lack of available space, I placed him with two much smaller puppies for company close to the house. The following morning when I went to see him, he looked drowsy, and I suspected that he may have experienced yet another seizure. Just in case he had, I took him to the house and put him in a cage where he could be warm and calm and safe from attack from the other puppies, where I could be with him twenty four hours a day.

That evening the seizures began again, and he was having a seizure every twenty minutes. Indeed he was only waking up to have another seizure. They were becoming more violent, with his mouth opening and snapping closed and his long legs moving rapidly as if he was in a race. I telephoned George to ask how much of the calming medication I could safely give him. One tablet is usually enough to calm a dog that weighs between ten and twenty kilograms. Peter was a mere five kilograms, and yet one tablet had very little effect on him. I then remembered that I had some Valium, which I could I administer rectally, and the two medications had a slight calming effect on him. He was exhausted after several hours of seizures, and so it was that night we both slept soundly in the armchair. The following day Peter seemed a lot better and only experienced a couple of seizures, which I seemed to be able to control with the medication. But as I removed him from his box, I realized that he could not see anything. He rushed about the room bumping into the furniture and becoming more and more distressed. When I took him outside so he could urinate, the unfamiliar surroundings made him panic even more. His four long legs were then flaying about, and as I attempted to pick him up, one of his long legs caught the corner of my mouth and the side of my face. His sharp claw gave me a nasty gash, which bled profusely. Now I looked like something from a horror film! *Nice face for Christmas,* I told myself with my usual sense of black humour as I looked in the bathroom mirror.

George was, as always, his helpful self, and despite it being Christmas, we kept in regular telephone contact. He even offered to take Peter into the clinic, but I would not allow this to happen as the poor man really did deserve some sort of break. The results of Peter's blood test revealed lots of conflicting factors, but I gave him the antibiotics that were recommended by George, and Peter gradually improved. He was eating well, but still he could not see, and when he was outside in the open space, he tended to panic. Yet in a confined space, he repeatedly bumped into everything, and this also upset him. After a few days of taking him outside onto the verandah, Peter began to recognize the area, and he seemed to be coping better with his loss of sight, although he was still hyperactive. Gradually over the coming days, I realized that he was seeing objects, and although he was still rather clumsy, at least he was not walking head-on into them. A few weeks passed, and I was able to put Peter outside again. Initially I kept him apart from the other pups as the danger of him having another seizure amongst them was too great a risk to take. For certainly he would inevitably have displayed the sort of behavior that they would not have been able to recognize, and then the other pups would possibly have attacked him. But as the days and weeks passed, Peter had no further attacks, so I was able to place him with some pups who were much younger and smaller than he was.

Later, Peter received his routine vaccinations with no apparent ill effects. He played with the younger pups, and he was such a gentle and loving dog, who never bullied them or took their food, so I was hopeful that one day someone would want to offer him a home. Whilst he had had no further seizures, George told me that there was always a possibility that he could develop epilepsy at some stage in his life. Then in September 2008, Peter was put on the German Web site for re-homing. Finally, a wonderful German family offered him a home. On Sunday, 21 September, Peter left Crete to start his new life in Germany.

At the same time as all these events were happening with Peter and Santa, Colin is asked by an old man at the *kaffenion* if he would take a look at his donkey, whose name is Jannie. Through an interpreter, the old Cretan man tells Colin that the donkey is not eating, and he thinks that he may have a problem with his teeth. Over the preceding five years, Colin has acquired quite a reputation among these tough Cretan men of the village for his willingness to help out in whatever way he can, repairing their tools and pulling their cars out of the olive groves when they get stuck. But more importantly they respect his knowledge and familiarity with all animals and in particular with horses and donkeys. With no local farrier available, Colin has had to trim our donkeys' feet and trim and shoe our two horses whenever necessary as well as regularly trimming the overgrown feet of the donkey who belongs to the village taxi driver's wife and still works carrying food for their other livestock.

Colin goes to have a look at the donkey, and when he returns home, he suggests that I go with him as he fears that the poor animal may have tetanus. Sure enough, the donkey has a small cut behind his ears, which was most probably caused by a chaffing head collar. The stable, although dry and with a deep bed of straw, has possibly never been cleaned out, and it is deep with donkey droppings and stale urine. It also seems to double as a junk room with old metal bed parts everywhere. The donkey is hobbled by the front feet in the usual way. This also means that he is more likely to fall over on the uneven and small area that has been allocated to him, so we release him. Adonis, his owner, shows me the antibiotic that the local sheep vet has given him, and I realize that he has not given him any yet. So we clean up the wound and give the donkey his antibiotic. Jannie is clearly suffering from tetanus, and there is very little chance of him surviving. His body and limbs are rigid. His jaw is clamped shut, and he has had nothing to eat or drink for several days; they tell us. It is Christmas, the pharmacies and the vets are closed, and we have nothing with which to treat the poor animal. We visit him daily, and each time we do, we see that he has fallen to the ground. Getting him up onto his feet is difficult for the two of us, as he is heavy and rigid and unable to help himself, so Adonis's son gives us a helping hand. He speaks a little bit of English, so with my limited Greek and simple English, I warn him that the donkey's chances are minimal. I make a soup of powdered vitamins and crushed oats. Jannie is interested and tries his best to slurp it through his clamped jaws.

Finally I manage to get my long-suffering vet George on the telephone. He is open for a day, and so I visit him. He knows that I am usually pretty stoic, but with the lack of medication and knowledge, the sheer feeling of impotence overcomes me, and I burst into tears. "No one seems to care," I tell him. The local sheep vet had told me that Adonis had been to see him and that he had mentioned to him that the donkey had a cut on his head. The vet had then asked the old man if the donkey had tetanus, and the old man Adonis had said no! "How would he know?" I ask George. "One brief visit by the vet would have made the diagnosis, and then maybe, just maybe he could have been treated instead of being left to die a slow and lingering death."

George, as always sensitive and ready to listen, becomes motivated to try and help me, and he gives me a prescription for the anti-tetanus serum tetagum. He explains to me how much I would need and that it is very unlikely that the pharmacist could get me the whole amount at once. He also gives me atropine and muscle relaxants and tells me what and how much to administer. Sure enough, we can't get all the tetagum that we need at one go, so I take what they can get for me and administer the other medicaments. The muscle relaxant and atropine have an almost immediate effect and enable the poor animal to move his legs a little and to relax his jaw sufficiently enough to drink copious amounts of fluid. We repeat this procedure twice a day for the following three days, making the daily trips to the pharmacist for the pre-ordered tetagum. I really hoped that we were making some sort of improvement for the poor beast.

Then on the morning of the fourth day, which was 24 December, we visited Adonis, and he told us that Jannie was dead. Both Colin and I felt so very low and so sad for the poor old donkey to have died in such a way. Oh, if only I had known more! If only the Cretans were not so fatalistic about their animals. If only the vets would explain to them that one yearly anti-tetanus vaccination would prevent all this suffering and death, especially when it is a known fact that there appears to be a high death rate from tetanus in the donkeys here on Crete. These poor animals who have served their masters and mankind faithfully for generations are so badly treated, neglected, and abused by the human race. *Why*, I ask, *are we so disrespectful and so abusive?* Why do we take so little care of beings that are unable to care for themselves? What sort of race are we? Does anyone really care about one sick donkey as they tuck into their Christmas dinners and booze and forget about the suffering under their own noses as they open their expensive, frivolous, and unnecessary gifts, forgetting that the most precious gift of all is *life*.

Tetanus

This is a neuromuscular disorder caused by a specific neurotoxin, which is produced by the bacterium *Clostridium tetani*. The organism is present in the soil and feces and can readily enter the animal's bloodstream through any small cut as in the case of dear Jannie.

The infected animal shows initial signs of stiffness and is often reluctant to move. Often his head and ears are extended. Mastication can be difficult, and the first signs that the owner may observe is the animal's reluctance to eat. When death occurs, it is usually due to exhaustion, poor circulation, and pneumonia, which is almost inevitable if the correct treatment cannot be administered quickly and effectively.

Eight | Dennis's Tail

IT WAS JUST another dirty cardboard box left outside the animal shelter on a balmy evening in September 2004. Inside it were four dirty, fluffy bundles who were visibly teeming with external parasites. These four frightened, little puppies were aged about four weeks old and far too young to have been taken away from their mother. The isolation unit in the animal shelter was already too full, and so Ines the vet telephoned me to ask if I could possibly accommodate them all. My small puppy isolation area was already full, but there was space in the horses' stable at the moment as Arnie preferred to be left out in the field these days. For the time being, they could make use of his stable. Ines sent a volunteer with the tiny puppies and promised to visit us the next day to check them all over.

As usual the vets were inundated with work, often starting at the animal shelter before seven in the morning and leaving around midnight the same day. It was time to use the letter D, so Dennis, Daphne, David, and Delia were all duly named. They were treated with parasitic spray and given their doses of worming cream. Four hungry, little mouths eagerly devoured their meals of puppy chow and puppy meat, after which they instantly settled down to sleep in their small kennel inside the stable. The following morning I discovered the usual pile of spaghetti-type roundworms that had been shed by each of these little creatures. Obviously their mother had never been wormed and had managed to pass the parasites onto her pups, who in turn had never been wormed. This is normal here on Crete, and I never cease to be amazed at the quantity of long white worms that even the smallest puppy has been carrying in his/her intestines. The puppies thrived in their new environment, and all of them looked so appealing with their cream- and golden-colored, dense fluffy coats, *which would serve them well,* I thought, *when they reached their new homes in Germany in the coming months.*

Colin had gone to England for his annual summer break, so I had a friend named Linda staying with me in the house to help with the work and the stray animals, who were steadily increasing on a daily basis. Gradually we were running out of available space, pens, and kennels in which to keep the number of puppies that were coming our way. They were invading my hotel guest area, and this was becoming a bone of contention between Colin and me, as we needed the hotel spaces to be kept available for our paying guests. After all, this was our main source of income. One week later all four small puppies seemed to be eating well enough, and they did not appear to have any obvious signs of illness, so they were able to be transferred from the stable into the small puppy compound close to the house.

It was just a few days after their move that I was woken up at four o'clock in the morning by the sound of squealing and yelping coming from the direction of the puppy area. Instinctively, as I have previously mentioned, you learn to differentiate between the numerous sounds, the play bark, the bullying bark, the testing bark, the injured yelp, and the frantic cry. This was a frantic cry, and my initial thoughts were that one of the smaller and weaker pups was being attacked by one of the larger ones. Outside it was still very dark and cold, and my friend Linda had also woken up. She too was worried about the sounds that she had heard. I reached for the torch beside the bed, grabbed my dressing gown, rushed outside, hastily put on freezing-cold Wellington boots on bare feet, and ran over to the puppy compound. By now there were about fifteen small puppies racing up and down the confined area. They were all yelping and squealing with excitement, a sure sign that all was not as should be at that time in the morning.

I shone my torch along the fence line where the majority of the puppies seemed to be congregated, and there on the ground I could see the small golden-colored puppy who I now knew to be Dennis. He lay on the icy cold earth, twitching and shaking and making no attempt to get up. My initial thought was that he had been attacked and was now badly injured, shocked, and unable to move. Quickly I scooped him up in my arms and carried him back to the house where I could examine him to see the extent of his injuries. Wrapping him in a clean towel and expecting to see signs of blood, I searched his wet and now very cold body for injuries, but I could find none. Looking at his face in the dim light of the oil lamp and torches, I realized that his eyes were rolling upward. His small limbs were still shaking, and he had what resembled a snarl as his lips retracted and he opened and closed his mouth. It was obvious to me now that Dennis was having an epileptic seizure. The seizures lasted about twenty seconds and occurred at half-hourly intervals.

In those early days of animal protection and having the constant support of the German vets, I had no supply of medication in the house. So wrapping him in a warm blanket, I decided to sit with him on my lap and wait until daylight, when I felt that I could phone the vets, not wanting to call them at that unearthly time in the morning, knowing that they probably did not get to bed until well after midnight. At about seven in the morning I telephoned Ines, who came to our place immediately and gave Dennis a mild tranquilizer. Sadly he failed to respond and his condition remained the same, so she set up an intravenous infusion hoping that he would now improve and thus avoid having to take him to the animal shelter where his life would be in even more danger from infection or from the many puppy viruses that were a constant problem among the small creatures and in the main responsible for the majority of the puppy deaths.

Virtually all of the pups in the animal shelter have been born to sick and malnourished mothers who for sure have never been vaccinated, and therefore the puppies are often fragile little creatures. Having been removed from their mother before they had a chance to build up their immune system, they are vulnerable to every bacteria and virus they come into contact with, and of course in any animal shelter, these are everywhere.

Sadly Dennis's seizures did not stop, and his life was in imminent danger, so the only remaining option was for him to be taken to the animal shelter where he could be cared for by the vets despite all the other risks involved.

In early October and by November the vets were telling me that Dennis's condition had not improved, and he was still experiencing numerous seizures on a daily basis. To make matters even worse for him, he now appeared to have suffered some degree of brain damage as a result of the recurring seizures, and this had resulted in him becoming blind. His small body was covered in abscesses from the numerous injections, and there really was very little hope that he was going to make a good recovery. It was certainly going to be very difficult if not impossible to find him a home in Germany with so many problems, even if he did survive.

On my next visit to the animal shelter, I went to see Dennis, and I was shocked to see him sitting alone in a metal cage. It was obvious that he was unable to see anything, and his little head kept turning from right to left in an attempt to follow the sound of my voice and then in another direction whilst he was trying to make sense of the numerous sounds in the noisy shelter. He looked so vulnerable and insecure, and my heart went out to him, but back at home I was inundated with small puppies, and I did not feel that I could cope with him and all his problems as well. By the end of November the vets were telling me that Dennis's epilepsy has been stabilized, and all he now required was one small tablet to be given to him every evening. Unfortunately he remained blind, and despite putting his details on their German Web site for re-homing, no one had come forward or even shown any interest in him.

I still had the awful image of him in my mind sitting alone in the metal cage, confused and insecure. So after a brief discussion with Colin, we decided that Dennis would be better off here with us and that somehow we would cope. We thought that he would soon adapt and learn where everything was. The vets agreed that he could come back to us as he was now fully vaccinated and he seemed to be improving every day. Then just a few days before he was due to arrive to live with us, Mike the vet told me that he believed that Dennis had regained some of his eyesight, more in one eye than the other, but that he seemed to be adjusting to this and managing even better, as clearly now he could see something. So Dennis came home and he was allowed to sleep in the house with our own dogs Zak and Charlie, who as older dogs, were not too keen on having a pup around the place. But Dennis soon learned where his boundaries were.

He took his daily medication in a piece of soft cheese, and there were no signs of his epilepsy recurring. In March the vets suggested that I attempt to reduce his medication, which I did without any ill effects on his behalf. Later I was able to stop it altogether, and Dennis was fine, and to this day he has never had another seizure. His sight, whilst not one hundred percent, has slowly improved over the past four years, and he is a happy and confident little dog. Whilst he remains the smallest dog we have, he has the role of the family watchdog and policeman, barking at the slightest noise and movement outside, but unfortunately always fails to stop doing so even when he is told.

In 2009 Dennis is still thriving, although I am sorry to say that he does have one major downfall, which everyone staying at our home overnight needs to be made aware of, and that is that Dennis is a compulsive sock thief who can be heard tiptoeing into any bedroom at all times of the night in search of his desired object. Once he has acquired his trophy, he quickly scurries out, and if observed, he will put the entire sock inside his mouth to hide it, thus managing to convince the inexperienced sock owner that they must be mistaken. However once outside the house and frequently some considerable distance from it, Dennis will deposit his prize, rather like a squirrel depositing his nuts in a safe place, so that he may retrieve them at some time in the future. Before Dennis's little fetish was discovered, his compulsion had caused a certain amount of domestic disharmony between Colin and myself, as I was frequently accused of losing one of each of his pair of socks in the washing process. It was not until Colin was out walking Leo, our rescued Belgium Shepherd dog, in the lane near our home one morning that he stumbled across a larder of no less than twelve odd socks, which he quickly recognized as his own, neatly stashed in a pile in the roots of an old orange tree. Since then, every unsuspecting visitor to our home has needed to be warned that when they remove their dirty socks, they really do need to place them well out of Dennis's reach or to bear the consequences. To observe the bleary-eyed visitor who has failed to heed my warning emerge from the bedroom in the morning with a rather puzzled and confused expression, only to tentatively ask me with a certain degree of embarrassment if I had seen one of their socks, usually sends me into a convulsive set of giggles and for Dennis to retreat to the nearest chair, knowing full well that he is in big trouble.

Nine | Amber's Tail

I WAS DRIVING past Kostas's place on my way to the local feed merchant with Roy, the wonderful guy who had magically cured my horse Arnold's torn ligaments in his neck by using acupuncture. In doing so, he had fully restored my half-dead friend back to full health in less than one week, but I digress as that is another tale. We heard Kostas's distinctive voice calling, "*Ella,* Freida, *ella,*" which sounded more desperate than just a social greeting. So we drove into his place, which can be a hazardous exploit in its self due to the half-buried car parts, pieces of old tin roofing, and long-forgotten rotting pieces of wood and mangled wire. What first caught my eye was a spray can containing some lethal Cretan concoction (which I now know to be a mixture of diesel and water), which Kostas held in one hand whilst with the other hand he was pulling a long length of dirty, fraying rope from an equally dirty one-time blue plastic barrel precariously balanced on a pile of rotting wood several feet off the ground. After a couple of tugs there emerged a beautiful, amber–colored, German shepherd-collie cross bitch, thin and shaking yet somehow managing to look dignified in these very undignified surroundings. As he pulled her further out of the barrel, pups cascaded from her, dropping onto the soft ground below. They seemed to be everywhere, crying and flaying around helplessly. There were in fact eight small brown and black blobs, possibly only a few hours old. Their eyes and ears sealed, they were helpless and confused as they thrashed about and squealed in the long grass.

Kostas started to spray the bitch with the concoction, so using my very limited Greek, I tried to intervene. But looking at the dog, I realized why he was using such drastic measures. This poor animal was covered in ticks; her eyelids, lips, ears, in fact everywhere I looked on her body appeared to have these huge creatures hanging from her, which were a dark purple in color and gorged with her blood. Clearly as a stray, she had been living in a heavily contaminated field for some time. Kostas told me that he had discovered her that morning in a nearby olive grove on the edge of the village of Armenoi. He also made it clear to me that he did not want her (*Thank goodness,* I thought to myself) as he has enough work to do looking after his pigs and goats, of which he appeared to have at least ten, plus some sheep and a conglomeration of other animals including various dogs tied up on short chains to a variety of abandoned vehicles.

Roy hastily gathered up the tiny, helpless pups and placed them in a tattered old box that he had found nearby in the rubbish. As he placed the box on the back of my pickup truck, this lovely bitch was getting increasingly agitated and straining at her rope collar in an attempt to reach her little family. She looked shocked and anxious as we bundled her onto the pickup next to her pups, so Roy climbed onto the back and sat beside her whilst we drove the short distance back to our place. Not being too sure at that time exactly what Kostas has sprayed her with, I decided to sponge her down with lukewarm water, lest it be harmful to her pups. She put up no resistance and sat patiently on the back of the pickup truck until I had finished. It was only then that Roy and I realized the horrifying number of ticks that were on her body, and Roy with his lifelong experience of horses and dogs on three continents had never before seen such an infestation. For the next half hour, we laboriously removed hundreds of the hideous creatures before placing her and the pups in their makeshift home. Somehow I just knew that this dog was going to be special. Despite her obvious vulnerable situation, she looked at me with a mixture of fear and trust, striking a chord deep in my soul that I knew would stay with me forever. Sometime later, after being fed and watered and suckling her eight pups, she looked a picture of contentment despite her boney frame protruding through her long, amber coat.

When Ines, the German vet from the animal shelter visited the next day, she examined Amber and noticed that her gums and whites of her eyes were in fact a bright yellow color, which she diagnosed as the signs of liver damage, possibly due to the birth and rather like the condition of eclampsia, often found in human mothers and that can be fatal. This beautiful bitch was indeed lucky to be alive. We were unable to vaccinate her because of her condition, and she was given a special diet to support her liver. Ines also thought that we should try to foster some of her pups, as possibly eight were going to be too much for this malnourished and sick mother to feed and care for. There was also the very real possibility that she might not fully recover either, so Ines brought Beth, who was a young healthy mother with only one surviving pup out of three.

I placed Beth and her huge pup in the adjoining kennel, and I left a towel for Beth and her pup to sleep on overnight. The following morning I managed to smuggle three of the sickly mother's pups into Beth's den without, I thought, either dog realizing what I had done, having first rubbed the pups all over with the towel to ensure that they smelled like their new foster mother and her cub. Whilst this was a way of ensuring that the pups would survive, even if their mother didn't, I couldn't help but feel as if I was robbing this young mother of her little family. I also believe that she knew exactly what I was doing, as at a much later date, perhaps a matter of several weeks later, with the two mothers living in such close proximity to one another, I discovered this beautiful and highly maternal bitch feeding one of her previously removed pups, which had somehow managed to squeeze himself under the dividing gate and back to his original mother.

I knew that this sickly young mother was really something special, so I decided to call her Amber, which was the color of her coat. She was also proving to be an excellent mother, feeding her pups and keeping her den meticulous despite her own fragile condition. Unlike her neighbor Beth, who really was a sloppy sort of mother and barely able to clean up after one pup let alone the four that she now had! Amber was also a fiercely protective mother, and whilst she would allow me to do anything that I wanted to do with her and her offspring, the same could not be said of her reaction to my husband Colin, whom she repeatedly tried to attack and succeeded in biting three times on the backside after he turned his back on her! Clearly she was not happy around any man, so who knows what she had suffered in the past?

I have found this to be a common pattern of behavior of many stray dogs, as it is usually the Greek men who issue the punishments. But what I have found even more surprising is that even some of the very young puppies, who arrived here when they were just a few days or weeks old, have this same built-in fear of men. Surely they could not have learned this in such a short period of time, so I have come to the conclusion that perhaps after hundreds of years of mistreatment, this message has in some way been passed from mother to her offspring.

Amber remained skinny despite the huge amounts of food she was consuming. She was treated for her numerous parasites, and her blood samples were taken and sent for analysis. Still she managed to cope with her brood despite debilitating bouts of diarrhea. Her personality shone through, and she and I became as one as she obeyed my every command without question and intuitively knew what I wanted and how I was feeling. Weaning her pups as they grew became another problem, as Amber had known starvation, and she would always eat anything and everything that was put in front of her. So putting food down for her pups at feeding time just meant more for her. Despite her strong maternal and protective instincts, not one of her pups would even dare to look at the food lest she attacked them. So fearing that I was going to have several pups with eating disorders, who already scurried away to the furthermost corners of the compound when food arrived, I was left with no alternative other than to remove Amber at feeding times. And that solved the problem.

I was still unable to vaccinate her because of her yellow mucous membrane, her frequent high temperatures, and her perpetual hyperactivity, so she remained with us, and her future seemed uncertain. Her puppies were eventually weaned successfully, and all found homes in Germany. Still Amber retained her innate mistrust of the male species and would often try to bite the most inoffensive of men when they weren't looking. This also meant that re-homing her in Germany was not going to be an option unless the biting stopped. Over the coming weeks, I managed to persuade Colin without too much difficulty to allow her to stay with us, despite her numerous attacks on him, as I simply couldn't bear the thought of her and I being separated.

Eventually she was well enough to be spayed, and so two years later Amber was a beautiful, active, obedient, loyal, and loving dog to me. We had a rapport that I have never experienced with any other dog, despite the hundreds of dogs who have passed through my hands. My only sadness at this time was that despite our bond, she remained terrified of entering the house, and whilst she would venture just inside the door, any attempt to close it made her panic and run. She also remained suspicious of all men, and I suspected that this would never leave her. She was free to wander the garden and surrounding area, but she never left my side and laid on the doormat when I was inside the house.

One very hot day, Ines the vet insisted that she be allowed to take Amber to the nearby river to cool down. On arrival at the river, she took Amber into the refreshing mountain water believing that she would enjoy the treat. But Amber had other plans, and at the first opportunity she pulled Ines so hard that, despite the vet's fitness and strength, the poor girl fell over, facedown in the icy water. Amber, free at last, headed straight for home followed by a very wet and cold young vet! Amber's passion for food remained, which meant that she had to be fed far away from the other dogs for fear of her attacking them. But I loved her dearly, and the relationship that we had I would never have thought possible between human and dog, and it was indeed a privilege to have her in my life.

Amber's Death

It took me eighteen months to be able to write about Amber's death, and even now I am unable to read this chapter without shedding copious amounts of tears.

20 June 2006. Just a few days before this date, I had purchased new flea collars for all my dogs. As Amber was sprawled out on the cool tiles of the verandah, I decided that I would groom her and replace her old flea collar. I can recall that day as if it were only yesterday, enjoying the sheer pleasure of grooming her long amber coat. I can remember cupping her gentle face in my hands, putting my nose close to hers, and telling her how much she was loved as she stared into my eyes. In those days I always imagined that as Amber was so young, possibly only about three years old at the most, that the two of us would have many happy years ahead, and that she would still be with me into my old age.

Seated on the verandah, I was bottle-feeding yet another motherless pup who had been found in the rubbish, and Amber, who had never lost her strong maternal instinct, was curious about the little creature, constantly wanting to sniff and clean him as she had done so many times before. In yet another attempt to coax Amber into the house, I went indoors with the pup, knowing that she would follow me. Talking reassuringly to both of them, I seated myself close to the open door so that I could very gradually push it closed with my foot once I had got her inside. I had almost succeeded when Amber turned, and with that oh-so-familiar look of panic in her eyes, she ran outside. Putting the puppy down, I went to reassure her again and gently stroked her head. Oh, if only she could talk to me, what horrors she would reveal about her earlier experiences that have left her so very afraid of being trapped inside a house. As I could not persuade Amber to sleep inside the house, which I would dearly have loved, she slept with two of our other dogs in a dog house, which had a large compound attached and was positioned next to the stables and feeding room.

The routine was simple in those days. Every morning I would walk down the pathway from the house, and Amber would be waiting for me at the gate of the compound in order to be let out to join me in my daily chores. Every evening she would be fed nearby my other dogs, as finally she was beginning to eat her own food with out attacking the others. At long last she was starting to realize that there was always food in abundance for her. June 20· 2006, was a beautiful Cretan summer's morning, and I was in no particular hurry. There were no vet's appointments to keep, and I was not expecting any visitors. The dog and cat hotel was not too full, so I had no need to rush about for a change. So with this relaxed frame of mind, it did not strike me as odd that all my dogs were inside and not waiting at the gate to be let out. For some reason, having not seen them there, I began my usual work routine.

I had probably been working for about one hour when I realized that it felt strange not to have Amber at my side. Opening the gate to the compound, I expected all three dogs to come rushing out of the large kennel to greet me, but when none of them arrived, I was momentarily puzzled and went further inside to investigate. Bobby, our rather overweight rottweiler, was sitting at the back in his usual place. Little Wolf, our rescued part husky with her one blue eye and her one blue and brown eye, was sitting beside him. In front of them both lay Amber in her usual place with her long graceful body blocking the doorway, so the door could not be closed without her waking. At first glance she looked to be sleeping, and I wondered why she didn't move or respond to her name. I called her name again, and I really expected her to get up and wake from what must surely have been a very deep sleep. But there was no movement. Then I knelt down beside her, touched her now stiff body, and realized to my horror that she was dead. Immediately I turned to the other dogs, thinking that one of them must have killed her. They looked at me as confused and bewildered as I was. Then I ran my hands all over her body looking for signs of injury, but I could find none. There was no evidence of bleeding and no bitten tongue and no vomit. It was just as if she had died in her sleep. Bobby and Little Wolf remained where they were, as if they too were shocked, and they too could not understand what had happened to her.

A sense of panic came over me, and I screamed and cried as I have never done before or since. I cried uncontrollably, and I felt sick and dizzy; I was clearly in a state of shock. Could I have saved her if I had gone in to see her a little earlier? *Why Amber?* I kept on asking myself. Slowly I eased her long stiff body inside the kennel and told the other two dogs to leave us alone. I closed the door, and I sat there on floor beside her, holding her in my arms. I cried and sobbed so much that I thought that I would never be able to stop, and I honestly cannot remember very much about the rest of that day, only a feeling of shock, anger, total disbelief, and uncontrollable tears. I can remember just how horrible I was to all the other dogs by saying out loud, "Why couldn't it have been one of you instead of my beloved Amber?"

Two and a half years later the tears were still flowing. How I miss her as if it were only yesterday. Since that time I have cared for hundreds of dogs, and yet not one of them has ever reached that part of my soul that Amber reached. There have been times when I have been given a pup or a dog who in some small way resembles my beloved girl, in maybe the shape of her head or a certain mannerism or a touch of the color amber in the coat, and I dearly wish that he or she could be my Amber reborn and sent to me to care for. But like I keep on saying, there are no fairy-tale endings in the world of animal protection, not on Crete anyway. Amber was buried in a corner of our garden close to the house where I can sit and talk to her and tell her about my day.

Sadly since then there have been many puppy deaths over the years, and each one of them is buried close to my beloved Amber, who I know will be caring for them in the spirit world and where I know one day that we two will be reunited, when once again I can gaze upon her beautiful and trusting face and cup her head in my hands and tell her just how much she was loved and just how much she meant to me in the short time that we had together. I never knew what Amber died of; perhaps it was some hidden condition that was as a result of her poor physical state when she was found. She certainly never showed any symptoms of any other illness. She never appeared to be in any pain. I asked the vet about the new flea collar that she was wearing, and he assured me that this could not be responsible for her death, as she had worn one before. Unless she had eaten it, there was no possibility of it doing her any harm. So I am left not knowing exactly why she died and with the sadness of her loss, which will never leave me, but with the joy that I had known her, as without her in my life, I would never have thought it was possible to form such a lasting bond with any animal. But sadly the pain of her death remains as if it were only yesterday.

Ten | Kostas's Place

MANY TIMES IN this book I have made reference to Kostas and his place. To be able to do justice to our dear friend is difficult, unless you have some insight into the Cretan people, which in my opinion are like no other race I have come across. Hopefully by the time you have read this book, you will have a clearer understanding of them than we had when we first came to live here.

Kostas is in his mid–fifties, but he could so easily pass for thirty-five to forty-five with his full head of black curly hair only just showing signs of greying and his soft sensual brown eyes. He is about five feet, six inches tall, very slim and wiry, and usually sports a short goatee. In his youth, Kostas was a very good football player and still maintains that athletic persona. I am sure that he has never left the island of Crete, and I suspect that he has not even been to the capital Heraklion some one hundred fifty kilometers away from Armenio, where he was born and where he still lives in the same house. By most people, he is considered a harmless rogue, although there are stories that in his youth he was often threatened by jealous Cretan husbands for flirting with their wives. But this is Crete and very much a male-dominated society still. Kostas appears to be antiestablishment and works as a self-employed plumber, supplementing his income with his production of goats' milk, breeding and rearing pigs for slaughter, and with the occasional sale of hunting dogs or peacocks, and any other projects that come his way, which he jokingly calls "business." He has never been married, and I do not think that he ever will get married, even though he can be very charming. He has been a good friend to us from the time that we arrived. He appears not to be able to speak any English, although I suspect that he can understand some words of many languages, which he has told me that he learned from his many tourist girlfriends over the years. Kostas was certainly quick to recognise how useless and corrupt our house builders were, and evidently he insulted them on a daily basis on our behalf unbeknownst to us. He is always prepared to help out in a crisis and has frequently called upon Colin to help him with his succession of broken-down motorcars and vans, all of which have been death traps and frequently have no hand brake or even the basic requirements for the average motorist.

As I said, Kostas was born in the village of Armenio. I believe that he was the second youngest of four boys whose father tragically died when they were all very young. With no financial support available from the government for his mother and no close extended family in the village to help her, she had to make an impossible decision about how many and which of her children she could keep with her and which ones would need to

be fostered. I understand that one of the boys was sent to a relative living in Athens, and one was sent to live with someone in the nearest town of Chania, whilst his mother struggled to raise Kostas and his older brother by earning money cleaning other people's houses and doing what she could. I find it hard to imagine the magnitude of his poor mother's loss, to first experience the tragic death of a husband, then to have to decide which of her precious boys she could keep and which to give away.

In Cretan culture, the man really is the head of the household, and so many religious and social rituals are led by him. Boys are taken to the *kaffenion* by their fathers at a very early age. The *kaffenion* is primarily a male establishment, and there they are initiated into the ways and rites of their culture and village life in particular. As Kostas and his brothers grew, I imagine that they must have felt at an enormous disadvantage without a father as a role model and a provider. Also as males, they would all too soon have felt the responsibility of having to care for and protect their mother.

In Crete, the land is often jointly owned by the female members of the family, and it is usually handed down from generation to generation as a sort of dowry. This can mean that several female members of a family may jointly own one piece of land in the same way that several male members may jointly own one property. This explains why you can see so many old and neglected properties all over the island. When a property has been left to several individuals, obviously they all have to agree to either maintain it or sell it. In these modern times, the respective owners may have emigrated to America, Australia, or New Zealand, all of which were popular destinations in the early 1960s for the young Cretan man looking for a better future. Families drift apart, and disagreements are easy where money and property are concerned. As a result, nothing gets done, and the once much-loved family home falls into ruin.

I have been told that Kostas's mother inherited a piece of land when her husband died that is also jointly owned by her sister-in-law Aphroditi, who spends six months of the year living in America and five months of the year living in Athens, only returning to the family home in Armenio for the month of August, when it is traditional for all the family members to return to their village homes to celebrate married Maria's name day on 15 August. So in the intervening periods, Kostas has free reign to the piece of land, much to Aphroditi's distress at times; I have observed.

The piece of land that I have referred to as Kostas's place is approximately two minutes' drive away from our home. It measures about one *stremma* and stretches from the boarders of the agricultural road to a fast-flowing river at the rear. The freezing-cold river is bordered by tall mature trees, which serve as a welcome canopy in the hot Cretan sun. Under the shade of the trees, Kostas has built himself a hospitality area on a wooden platform that spans the fast-flowing mountain water that runs beneath. On top of this wooden platform, he has erected a wooden hut, which serves as a bedroom on hot, barmy, Cretan nights when perhaps after consuming too much of the local wine and *raki*, he can fall into bed. We have spent many pleasant evenings at Kostas's place in his company along with some of his other friends who just happen to be passing this remote piece of land. It is somehow rather bizarre to be sitting on an old bus seat, which may or may not have been securely fastened to a makeshift wooden platform, which spans a freezing-cold river on a hot Cretan evening with the guarantee of being remorselessly bitten by mosquitoes. The river also serves as a cooler for his numerous bottles of the local brew of *raki* and village wine, these bottles having first been securely tied around the necks with a piece of string and lowered into the icy water only occasionally to escape and float away in the direction of Kalives and ultimately the blue Mediterranean.

He always has a variety of dogs, goats, chickens, and peacocks nearby and a selection of abandoned vehicles, which often serve as kennels for Kostas's latest acquisitions. I have taken several dogs from him over the years, the most important and most treasured was my dear Amber. It would appear, from what I can understand, that Kostas is always willing to take on a dog or a puppy who he has found or has been given to him from individuals who just want to get rid of the animal. I took one such female dog, who gave birth whilst we were there. She was chained to a small plastic barrel, which was not really large enough for her to get into, let alone the ten pups she produced. Her name was Liza, and I still have one of her pups with me one year later, as they were all problematic in a variety of ways and difficult to re-home.

Kostas does care about his animals, but he does not always seem to understand the need to give them regular food and water, and they are only too frequently fed on any leftovers he can acquire form the local taverners. On one earlier visit to Kostas, I recall him proudly showing us a box of small pieces of grey matter with which he was feeding the dogs, and on closer investigation, we realized that they were in fact a box of outdated, ex-naval emergency rations that were intended to be used for human consumption only under strict supervision and in times of emergency. No doubt his often very hungry animals would have devoured these dehydrated tablets and then drank copious amounts of water, which would inevitably have caused the ingredients to swell up in the animals' stomachs and intestines, no doubt giving the animal serious abdominal pain. We did our best to try to persuade Kostas that these tablets should not be given to any animal, but unable to communicate in Greek in those days, I am sure that our advice was ignored. So whenever we are given a supply of food from one of our German animal protection organizations, we always give Kostas some of it with strict instructions that the food is only to be given to his dogs and that it is not to be used for fattening up his pigs. In order to enable him to carry out our instructions, we also manage to acquire a sack full of stale bread from a bakery every week, which we deliver to him for his pigs. Cretan bread does not contain preservative when it comes directly from the local bakers, and it tastes like nothing else you have tasted before. However, when it becomes stale, it also becomes rock hard, which is no problem for the pigs, but only too often I have seen him also feeding this to his hungry "rescued" dogs.

By English standards of animal care, Kostas could possibly be prosecuted for keeping animals on short chains and with limited shelter, food, and water. But by Cretan standards, his level of care could be considered more than adequate. The dogs may be on chains, but this is quite acceptable here; they receive food and water, although this may not be daily. Generally with Kostas, they are safe from being poisoned or shot. However if he should decide that he does not want them any longer, he may well dispose of them by shooting them himself, which would at least be a quick death, unlike the death of many of the abandoned animals here on Crete.

Eleven | Flipper's Tail

IT WAS OCTOBER 2005, and Colin had just returned from his annual trip to England. My eldest son and his wife were due to visit us in the next few days, so we were actively cleaning and preparing the house in readiness for our visitors as well as trying to catch up with all the work outside. I am afraid that with so many animals to care for, the housework tends to be left until last. Colin was yet again loading up the truck with the many bags of animal excrement, empty food tins, and numerous other waste products that accumulate when you have so many animals to care for. Thankfully the local council garbage dump is only two kilometers away from the house, which is a great help.

When Colin returned, I heard the ominous beep from the truck horn, which always indicates that he has company on board, usually of the four-legged and furry kind. By the time that I got to the truck, I could see Colin gathering up a large bundle of brown fur. It never ceases to amaze me that this large burly carpenter, who has never been known to shy away from trouble in his youth, can be so gentle and kind, so patient and reassuring to all animals and especially those who are sick or injured. As

Colin walked toward me with the poor creature in his arms, I could plainly see that it had a large, oozing abscess in the center of its back, roughly measuring four inches in diameter. The wound was covered with dirt, flies, and congealed, foul-smelling blood and pus. Colin told me that this little brown dog was unable to stand up and appeared to be shivering from fear and cold or shock from the injuries that he had received.

Until recently we had always relied on the German vets who worked for the animal organization called Arche Noah Kreta to treat the many stray animals, but with their imminent departure from the island, I had started to make contact with the local Cretan vets. We had discovered a very kind, knowledgeable, and gentle vet called George Vizyrakis, who had a practice in the town of Souda. Colin took the little brown dog directly to George's veterinary surgery, and after the initial examination, George asked Colin if he wanted him to put the poor animal out of his misery. But Colin declined his thoughtful offer and told him that we would like to try and treat the little dog, if it were at all possible. So this gentle and reassuring vet incised the animal's wound on his back and drained about 250 ml of foul-smelling fluid. He then X-rayed the lower half of the little dog's back, and to his dismay, there were around one hundred pieces of gunshot, which could clearly be seen imbedded not only in his back but in his hind legs, tail, and feet. Pieces of shot could also be seen in every part of his hips and pelvic area. The most damaging of all were the two pieces that had lodged in his spinal cord, which had severed it and paralysed him. Obviously someone had driven this little dog deep into the center of the vast municipal garbage dump, a place where no one would see him, and he had shot the little animal at point-blank range, leaving him in agony and distress without even the courage to kill him completely.

October is the start of the hunting season here on Crete. I say this loosely because really there is nothing left to shoot anymore except small birds, such as sparrows. So the "hunters," dressed like Rambo and with enough ammunition to kill a herd of elephants, often resort to shooting the occasional cat, or as happened last year, when the hunters near our home had finished for the day, their own dog, leaving it in the road. Whoever had shot this little dog would have felt confident in the knowledge that there were no houses near the garbage dump, and another shot ringing out would go unnoticed. In addition the coward who did this deed must have felt reassured by the fact that every few days a huge bulldozer arrives at the dump to push all the waste products to the epicenter. This little brown dog would have been buried alive. George gave him an injection of steroids and a long-acting antibiotic gave us instructions to repeat this together with vitamin B injections, whilst refusing to take any payment for all his work and medication.

As with many spinal injuries, there are numerous other dangers and complications that can arise, such as urine retention and subsequent kidney failure, pressure sores, and pneumonia, just to mention a few. Thankfully my son and his wife are both medical doctors, and when they arrived, they were a tremendous help by giving the little dog his injections, which he was none too pleased about. Back at home the only available place to keep the little dog safe from harm from the other dogs was in Arnie's stable, so we made him a comfortable area and surrounded him with hot-water bottles. He enjoyed his food, and he drank well, which were all good signs to aid his recovery.

During the estimated three days that the little dog had been left in the garbage dump, he had obviously barked himself hoarse, and now his attempts to bark sounded rather more like a seal than a dog, so he was jokingly referred to as Flipper. There are times when having a sense of humour does help me to cope with these awful situations. George had put Flipper's age at around six years, and there was evidence from his neck that he had previously worn a large collar, as this had rubbed his fur away over the years. The tips of his ears were black from fly bites, and his eyelashes were missing, all evidence that he had spent his days tied up or more likely chained. Flipper was not thin or starving, so at least he had been fed on a regular basis.

At the beginning of every day, I would carry him from his bed in the stable to the shade of a small olive tree in front of the house and sit him on a blanket. He has always been very sensitive to touch, and I suspect this is because of the pieces of shot, which I understand can be liable to move around in his body and cannot be removed. So if handled wrongly, Flipper would often try to bite me, as no doubt he was in considerable pain from time to time. Although small, Flipper has always been a stocky little dog, so this journey twice a day was quite an ordeal for both of us. The good news was that, although paralysed from the waist down, Flipper's bladder appeared to have an automatic empty device once it was full, which inevitably meant that he was unlikely to suffer from retention of urine and the subsequent complications of urine infections and kidney failure. However, he had no control over his bladder functions or the emptying of his bowels. This too made life even more difficult at times, as it was very important that we paid constant attention to him and moved him regularly to ensure that he was not left sitting for long periods in his own excrement.

A good friend and animal protector called Jayne Butler heard about Flipper's plight, and she sent numerous e-mails for me to many organizations, which she thought may be able to help him.

Kind individuals sent him small leather boots, which helped to stop his rear legs and feet from becoming skinned, raw, and infected, as he now attempted to drag himself around. Jayne then found Flipper the best gift of all. Suddenly she remembered that someone she knew had a set of wheels that had been donated a few years previously from an organization called Dog on Wheels in America. The little dog, who had benefited from the company's generous donation, now no longer needed the wheels. Jayne brought the wheels to the house, and they were almost the perfect size for Flipper. We gently fitted him into them, and within half an hour, he had mastered numerous techniques for getting around, quickly learning that he was able to reverse and do a three-point turn with ease. Now Flipper could easily outrun me and the other dogs with the use of his wheels. What a difference the wheels made to every one's life. Having them meant that he now went to the toilet as he walked along, and this in turn meant that he was no longer sitting on a wet and soiled blanket. His bladder emptied more frequently now as well, which was another positive advantage for his prognosis. Flipper's paralyzed feet and legs still trailed behind him, so the new shoes and boots were essential items, thanks to the kind and generous companies who sent them. This feisty little brown dog who had such a desire and will to live was now leading as normal a life as we could have wished for.

The only problems we encountered in those early days were his eagerness to explore his surroundings. At that time we had no main gate at the entrance to our property, so it was not too long before Flipper was trying to chase any passing vehicle. For the village people, being chased by a small brown dog is not so unusual. But to be chased by a small brown dog on wheels was something that they had never experienced or even thought was possible. I can remember on one occasion trying to catch up with Flipper, who had decided to pursue an elderly Cretan man making his daily visit on his motorbike to feed his pigs in a nearby olive grove. For a few moments, I had a vision of the poor motorcyclist coming to a tragic end as he turned his head to see who or what was barking at him. In doing so, the driver felt the need to do a double take when he saw it was not only a little brown dog but a little brown dog on wheels, travelling at top speed behind him. Unable to believe his eyes, the poor man veered off the road and narrowly missed having a head-on collision with a rather robust orange tree.

Our piece of land is agricultural, and it is surrounded by rather steep manmade ditches to help with drainage during the wet winter months. On several occasions, I found Flipper head-down in the watery ditch, and it was only the sounds of his distinctive bark and the sight of the metallic frame and rubber wheels protruding from the ditch that alerted me to his plight. The only alternative, we decided, was to fence off the entire garden and to make gates at the entrance for everyone's peace of mind. Colin was not a happy man.

On the day that Colin had discovered Flipper, we were all cautious about the little dog's life expectancy. Would it be hours, days, weeks, or months before he succumbed to the numerous possible complications that could be awaiting him? Not one of us could ever have imagined that four and half years later, and after a second set of wheels, that Flipper would still be living his life to the fullest. It was in those first depressing few hours when we really thought that we might have to put him to sleep, and as I was trying to go about my work, that I wrote this poem in my head and called it:

Little Brown Dog

Oh, little brown dog, with the face of an angel,
With eyes so pleading and hope eternal,
You have spent your long life chained up; that we know.
The fear in your eyes, it will never go.
Now we have found you midst rubbish and filth,
Deserted and paralysed, alone and in pain.
What brave human shot you
In the back at close range?
One hundred pieces of shot still remain.
What cowardly human did this deed to you,
Making sure he's not seen and well out of view?
Oh, little brown dog, with the face of an angel,
I curse him for you.
May he too suffer in pain and well out of view.
But I thank the spirits above that we found you.
For a few days at least, our love will surround you.
Your pain can be eased; your head can be stroked,

Your body caressed, and your wounds can be dressed.

Alas, little dog, your fate he has sealed.

Your legs will not move though your wounds may be healed.

Oh, little brown dog, with the face of an angel,

We must soon end your suffering forever.

But be sure you were loved, and we all tried our best.

You will die in my arms with your head on my breast.

Oh, little brown dog, with the face of an angel, rest in peace.

But in March 2006 . . . oh, little brown dog, with a face of an angel,

The strength of a lion and patience eternal,

We all thought your life had come to an end.

How wrong we all were, my strong little friend.

Though your back legs don't work, and they never will,

The wheels that we found you, they just fit the bill.

So now you can move with two legs and two wheels,

Up and down vale and even up hills.

You race all the dogs and overtake most.

If a girl is around, you are first at the post.

You look healthy and happy, and your tail wags with glee.

Oh, little brown dog, now your spirit is free.

In the past you have suffered, of that we are sure.

Yet your patience and tolerance and love are so pure.

Oh, little brown dog, with the face of an angel,

If only we humans had your trust eternal.

December 2007. Flipper is doing very well. His carriage has had numerous repairs. He can outrun almost any dog. He is fearless, happy, and affectionate. He will take on any opponent no matter what size they are, and if he detects that a female is in season, then he will guard her with his life. This had led to many problems for us in view of the fact that we are trying to run a cat and dog hotel, and customers do not take it too kindly when their unsuspecting pampered pooch is attacked by Flipper as he comes through the gate just because he might be a possible rival in love. For this reason, we had to make the decision to have Flipper castrated in order to save everyone from further injury.

The best news is that Flipper's back legs now have some movement. The wheels appear to have served as a daily form of physiotherapy. On a good day and when he is in the mood, Flipper can walk a short distance unaided, albeit his rear end looks somewhat drunk as he sways and waggles about. But he is a wonderful little character and quite a celebrity these days, an inspiration to us all. When the days are long and I am feeling tired and weary of all this animal protection, I look at Flipper's little brown face and trusting eyes, especially as he sleeps like a child at the end of another busy day. He always looks so peaceful and relaxed and I say, "Thank you, Flipper, for making me appreciate all the blessings that I have been given."

October 2008. Some time ago, I realized that Flipper's second-hand wheels were not going to last much longer. Colin had repaired them so many times, and wheel bearings had been replaced. The harness that secured him into his chariot had become so threadbare that now he needed to be tied into it every day. The tires were worn down to their last threads, and I could not even begin to imagine how Flipper or I would cope every day if he did not have any wheels. His quality of life would be drastically reduced, as he would insist on dragging himself around on the hard ground, and this would cause him excessive injuries. What is more, Flipper still does not like to be picked up, and he has a tendency to try and bite anyone who attempts to do so. In a moment of desperation, I took the liberty of e-mailing the company called Dog on Wheels in America, who had provided the first set of wheels, albeit for another injured animal. I told them Flipper's story and of our approaching difficulties, and to my absolute delight, Lori, the wonderful founder of the organization, replied to me immediately. Without a moment's hesitation, she offered Flipper a brand-new set of wheels, completely free of charge. Lori will never know how much relief, happiness, and quality of life they have given to Flipper and to me. The wheels arrived within the week by special delivery all the way from America to Crete, and they are a perfect fit due to the explicit chart that the company had sent me so I could measure Flipper accurately.

Please take a look at Dog on Wheels Web site to see what a wonderful job they do at www.doggon.com.

Twelve | Lazarus's Tail
(otherwise known as The Old Man)

IT WAS A Sunday morning in March 2007, and Colin was making one of his regular trips to the local council garbage dump, as usual taking with him several days' rubbish, consisting of empty meat tins, food bags, and the many plastic sacks of the excrement that are created by forty stray animals and one very busy dog and cat hotel. That day Colin was also taking some badly stained sheets and blankets that could no longer be washed by hand and needed to be disposed of, bearing in mind at that time, we still did not have electricity, and all our animals' blankets had to be painstakingly washed by hand. Thankfully I was helped in this strenuous work by my few conscientious volunteers.

It had been raining here for several days, and everywhere was muddy, grey, and foul. Every time I went outside to work with the animals, it meant a change of clothing, as the torrential rain seemed to penetrate the tightest seam and constantly ran down my sleeves and neck. Inside the house, it was dark and difficult to get anything dried. Without electricity even to brighten up the house, my spirits were low, and I wished for the rain to stop. The only good thing about the Cretan weather cycle is the fact that when it does finally stop raining, you can be assured of a few days of sunshine and warm breezes to dry up the ground, which can restore my energies and lift my spirits. But that day, as I recall, the rain showed no sign of abating; it was relentless. As Colin entered the drive on his return from the visit to the garbage dump, I heard the ominous toot from the truck's horn, his signal when he needs my assistance and usually because he has something onboard.

On my arrival at the truck, Colin leapt out of the driver's seat and went to the passenger door, carefully opening it. He stooped down, and from the foot well, he gently lifted out a small, filthy, and very wet little grey dog, which he had wrapped in some of the sheets that were intended for the dump. The little dog was about the size of a corgi and only appeared to be semi-conscious. Both his eyes were tightly closed, and one of them was oozing yellowy green pus, and his other eye was bleeding badly. His head looked swollen, and he was icy cold to the touch; we assumed that he must be very close to death. We found dry towels, and I quickly assembled the metal cage in the house and filled it with clean blankets and hot-water bottles. The little dog was still breathing, and yet he seemed to be unaware of what was happening to him, or he was too close to death to care.

Slowly I examined his frail little form; he was obviously a very old dog—more than that I could not say. Both his front legs looked bent, as if they may be broken, but then I assumed this was possibly due to chronic arthritis. I could not see any other injuries to his body, but his head and eyes looked dreadfully swollen. Colin had found him at the center of the garbage dump, and there was no possible way that this little dog could have got there on his own. Someone had obviously taken him there, and by the look of his injuries, they had attempted to kill him by hitting him about the head with an implement of some kind. From where he was situated, it was also possible that he had been thrown from the roadside. He had been left there to die a slow and what would have been an excruciatingly painful death in the freezing cold and torrential rain amongst the stinking refuse and rats.

Yet another victim of man's brutality, and he had been found close to the area where Colin had discovered Flipper just two years previously. It was a Sunday, and our dear vet George would not be in his clinic. So I telephoned the veterinary emergency number, but the vet on call was so very unhelpful, and his manner was so brusque and aggressive that I decided this little creature was unlikely to get good service from him. He would be better staying here with us until we could contact our dear George the following day. I cleaned the little dog's face and removed the large, red, leather collar from his small neck. The size of the collar would have been ideally suited for the neck of a rottweiler, but not, I remember thinking, for the once-delicate neck of this small canine. By the strain shown on the collar, he had obviously been chained up somewhere, probably for his entire life. The smell emanating from his fragile and bruised body was intense. He must had lain in the garbage dump for a considerable length of time, and the stagnant water from the refuse (which often consists of dead and half-dead pigs and sheep and the intestines of many animals), had washed over him.

We did our best to dry the little dog and surrounded his cold body with the hot-water bottles, blankets, and towels. In addition we lit the gas fire and put his cage close enough so he could feel the benefit from it for twenty-four hours a day. Thankfully he seemed unaware of what was happening to him, but *what a way,* I thought, *for him to end his probably already horrendous life. What sort of human being could do such a thing?* we asked ourselves. I offered him some food and water, and to our amazement, he rallied a little and drank a bowl full of fresh cold water and ate a little food with a degree of enthusiasm. He was too fragile to be bathed, and I considered that his delicate hold on life was far more precious than my rather oversensitive nose, and so we went to bed that night wondering if he would still be alive the following morning. Comforting ourselves that even if he was not, then at least he had died warm and cared for, in a degree of comfort, and not in that rat-infested and stinking garbage dump where his owner had intended him to die.

The following morning he was still very much alive, and his breathing was regular. His heart sounded strong, and he felt a lot warmer. Indeed the smell was intensifying with the assistance of the gas fire and the hot-water bottles. He had not urinated nor soiled his bed, so I carefully carried him outside and placed him on the ground. He was still rather confused, and of course despite having bathed his eyes, they were both still tightly closed, and he was unable to see where he was. He turned his head as if to bite me. Who can blame him? But I have learned that the only time I have ever been bitten by a dog has been when he or she has been afraid or injured, so I had a towel ready to put over his head in order to protect myself.

On the ground, although weak and unstable, he instinctively urinated, and then he allowed me to gather him up and to take him back indoors.

Today was Monday, so I telephoned George, our treasured vet, who of course without any hesitation told me to take the little dog straight there so he could examine him. George confirmed for me that the little chap, who was by now acquiring the name of The Old Man, did not have any fractures, and indeed his rather misshapen legs were the result of him having suffered for years from chronic arthritis. Without any painkilling drugs and undoubtedly having lived outside for his entire life, he must have experienced a lot of pain over the years. George was very shocked to hear how and where the dog was found, and he examined him so gently and with so much respect, as he does with all animals, whether they come from the richest of owners or from the street. When he examined the right eye, he showed me that it was badly infected because this poor little dog had recently suffered from a tooth abscess, which had formed a sinus erupting just below his right eye, filling it with pus. When George opened the left eye, we were both rather taken aback to find what looked like just the rear half of the eye, as if it had been completely sliced in half with a sharp knife. The only explanation possible was that when the despicable owner hurled this little dog into that horrendous garbage dump and so brutishly tried to end his life, the little dog must have landed on some sharp, protruding metal, and this had cleanly sliced off the front half of his eye.

One cannot begin to imagine the intense trauma that he must have felt, the hours of fear and confusion, cold, and distress that he must have endured, not only from the obvious beating in an attempt to end his life, but in addition from the never-ending pain that he must have had from the injured eye, inevitably left totally blind in a place that he could not have known and was unable to escape from, a place infested with rats, containing every possible item of refuse known to man, before Colin discovered him lying there almost unrecognisable as a dog. George had put his age at around sixteen or seventeen years, and he also noticed that the little dog had a badly deformed and twisted ear. I have seen this many times, and George told me that it is caused by the frequent twisting and bruising of the ear by the sadistic owner. In addition, he had cysts in this ear, which must have caused him a degree of deafness and further pain and discomfort.

George knows that I respect his professional judgements one hundred percent, and he respects my judgements as well. He knows that wherever possible, I would try to save an animal from further pain, and yet at the same time, I would want to give any animal every chance possible to end his or her days in comfort and with the dignity he or she so deserves as a living creature.

For example, some organizations will euthanize motherless pups who have been found with their eyes not yet open, which means they are less than two weeks of age. Thankfully I have never yet done this, and I have always managed to find willing volunteers to help me bottle-feed them, my opinion being that once an animal has been born into the world, then it has a right to life or a good try at it anyway. I believe that dogs like Flipper and now the poor Old Man have probably served their owners to the best of their ability over the years, and heaven only knows under what awful conditions they have probably lived. What meager rations they have been given and without any medical attention; that is for sure. Without any degree of respect or affection, the only thing that they could have been assured of was plenty of abuse and cruelty. Then when they are old and of no further use as potential guard dogs, or perhaps the owner just cannot be bothered to feed them any longer, or he just does not want them, he feels he has the right to dispose of them in any sadistic way that he should choose because no one will stop him or prosecute him or even be bothered to report him to the police. He remains safe in the knowledge that despite the laws that exist against animal cruelty, no action will be taken by the police or anyone else. This behavior revolts me, and I feel sick to my core when the owner does not even have the decency to ask a vet to terminate the animal's life with dignity and respect. Instead the already abused animal is subjected to a primitive and brutal death, or in the case of these two dogs, not even a speedy death but what would have been a slow and agonising death if they had not been found by Colin.

I strongly believe that there is an afterlife, a spirit world where we will all meet up one day and where we should all enter with a degree of dignity, if at all possible. So George and I discussed what we could do for the little animal. George administered a long-acting antibiotic injection and then suggested that I take him home, and in two week's time, if he was strong enough, then he could operate to remove the injured eye. Back at the house, the sun was shining, and the weather seemed a little warmer. The Old Man started to get restless in his confined area in the house. He was eating and drinking very well and appeared to be fiercely independent. So we put him out into the garden, and to everyone's delight, he started to walk about, mainly in ever-decreasing circles, but he could obviously see something from the eye, which was now free from infection. So he never bumped into anything, and we came to the conclusion that he could also hear a little bit. This Old Man seemed to be enjoying his days outside, and he appeared to be like a dog with a mission, as he never stopped walking around. At times this changed to a trot and then to a gallop. Maybe he was just enjoying his newfound freedom at long last. Who knows what he was thinking and what was going on in his mind as he paced about the garden? But for sure he did not like to be taken back in the house at night and confined in the metal cage, but this had to be done until his operation had been completed.

He still smelt awful, and his grey coat was stiff, matted, and foul to the touch, so we decided that he was now able to withstand a warm bath, which would surely make him and everyone else feel a lot better. I filled the bath with warm, soapy water, and Colin gently lowered him down into it. To our absolute amazement, he appeared not to mind this treatment at all, and gradually we saw the water turning to a dark greyish colour. This little dog was not a grey-haired dog at all but a beautiful snowy white one with delicate cream patches on his back. His hair was not coarse but as soft as cotton wool. He emerged from the murky water a completely different little dog, and he seemed to have really enjoyed the experience as much as we had. He now looked and smelled so much better after the removal of at least fifteen years of dirt, as well as the foul excrement in which he must have lain in the garbage dump for what George thought was least twenty-four hours.

The following week I had a trip planned to visit my grown-up children and granddaughter in England, so an animal-friendly couple called Rosemary and Colin offered to take care of the Old Man, as he still required rather a lot of work and supervision, and Colin had a lot to do without me at home. They took the little animal to George the vet for the operation to remove his damaged eye. All went very well, and they kindly looked after him post operatively for me until I returned home.

The weather was getting very warm now, so we gave him a kennel in the garden in the shade of one of the olive trees, and he quickly accepted this as his new home. Unfortunately he seemed to have very little sense of day or night, and he could be seen marching round the garden at midnight, which often caused chaos with all the other residents. In addition and on a more serious note, one morning I found him swimming in the ditch at the back of the house. Clearly he had managed to get through the very small gap in the gate and onto the road, and with his limited eyesight, he must have fallen into the deep ditch, which was filled with rainwater. I didn't know how long he had been there swimming around in circles, but clearly the time had come to make a small fence around his home so that he could be kept secure during the night or when we were away from the house. Throughout that summer he kept very well and seemed to be contented, quickly responding to the feeding routine. But during the cold and bitter Cretan winter nights, we took him indoors to sleep, which he was none too happy about. Lazarus came back from the dead, and the Old Man seemed to have done the same against all the odds. Everyone was delighted with his progress.

During 2008 he continued to live outside and continually marched around the garden like an old soldier; he bothered no one and no one bothered him. Even the dogs who were running free seemed to understand that he was old and not a threat to them. As the year progressed into April and May, we noticed a slight deterioration in his mental and physical state. Although he was still walking about, he now seemed to have lost the ability to reverse or to turn around. He often walked into corners or stationary obstacles, and then he would cry out for help as he was unable to find a way out or around it. This behavior was rather trying at times for me and dangerous for him, as in attempts to push his way through he often got himself trapped between gates and pieces of wood or underneath various items around the place. As the year passed and the months get hotter, he was starting to fall over a great deal, and there were times when he was unable to get up again.

Finally in July 2008, his situation rapidly deteriorated, and I discussed his problems with George, who agreed that maybe the time was getting nearer when we would have to put him to sleep. Then suddenly one very hot July morning, I noticed that the Old Man was spending more time falling over than he was standing up, and what was even worse now was there were flies following him everywhere. He was in very real danger of suffering from fly strike, a condition I have experienced with sheep in England. As any farmer will tell you, it is not a very pleasant demise for any animal as the flies and blue bottles settle on the animal and bury into their hair or wool, where they gradually break through the skin and start to lay their eggs under the surface. The eggs then turn into maggots, which in turn start to eat the animal alive.

So we knew without doubt that the time had finally arrived, and Colin and I took him along to the local vet in Kalives, as George was away at the time. With love and respect and with dignity, the Old Man was put to sleep in my arms in order to protect him from any further pain and misery. He had experienced sixteen months of the love and care that he had been denied in his previous sixteen years on this earth. He now experienced a calm and gentle death, which he was so rightly entitled to, in place of the slow and violent one that his previous owner had intended for him.

Thirteen | The History of Crete and Present-Day Attitudes to Dogs

IN AN ATTEMPT to understand the Cretan psyche and their attitudes to dogs, I feel that we first need to consider the unique geography and history of the island. Crete is a mountainous island that measures 156 miles (260 km) long and 34 miles (56km) at its widest point.

It has a character like no other, resembling the North and South of Europe and parts of Africa. Its weather conditions vary considerably within a few miles, and it has more than two thousand plant species, an immense variety of flora and fauna, where the cedar, palm, olive, orange, avocado, and banana trees grow side by side.

As recently as the twentieth century, the existence of King Minos and the Labyrinth was confirmed, and Crete was identified as the home of Europe's earliest civilization. Those initial inhabitants, the Minoans, are believed to have originated from Anatolia and to have led an extremely advanced and cultured society for almost five hundred years, from as early as 2000 BC.

It is recorded that it was then the Mycenaean Greeks took control of the island. Later the island passed from Greeks to Romans to Saracens and later to Venetians from 1204 up to 1669.

Throughout the Venetian period, the Cretan people suffered additional hardships and disasters, such as earthquakes, pirate raids, and crop failures. At the same time there were no less than twenty-two major epidemics of the plague, and entire villages were wiped out as their inhabitants succumbed to disease. During this period, you can also read about a life where the slave trade still existed, with slave markets being held in Heraklion. Attacks of piracy were commonplace, which forced the Cretan people to build their houses far away from the coastal areas, preferring to live close together for security and out of sight of marauding pirates. Finally the island's control was passed to the Ottoman Empire, in whose hands it remained until 1897.

Initially the Ottomans had been welcomed by the Cretan people, but it was not long before they too were imposing crippling taxes on the already-impoverished Cretan population.

But very little of the money paid in taxes was spent on maintaining buildings or roads, which then fell into disrepair. Everywhere there was overall neglect, and there was no encouragement for art, music, education, or any of the finer things in life. These were indeed hard times for the Cretan people, who worked hard for their rulers and yet lived in abject poverty. One way to seek favors from their Ottoman masters was to convert from Christianity to Islam (at least on the surface).

The population at this time is estimated to be about eighty

thousand inhabitants; fifty thousand of these were thought to be Christian, and thirty thousand were thought to be Muslim. This conversion to Islam brought many advantages to the Cretan individual, such as the right to own property and reductions in the taxes they had to pay. But the Cretan Muslims often continued to practice their Christianity in secret. Individuals who did not convert were increasingly repressed, and many took to living in the mountainous regions where Ottoman control was limited. So the mountainous regions became centers of rebellion, the first in the area known as Sfakia. Still today the mountain people of Sfakia are known for their fierce, proud, and irrepressible fighting spirit.

In 1770, the Cretan people were offered help from Russia, and an uprising took place, but the help was not forthcoming, and so the uprising was repressed. But this did not deter the feisty Cretan mountain people, and in the nineteenth century there were many more such bloody struggles. The year 1821 saw the Greek war of Independence, and the Pasha of Egypt, Mehmet Ali, was given control of Crete. It also brought more brutal campaigns, and again the islanders' resistance was crushed

In 1832 the independent Greek state was formed with the help of Britain, France, and Russia, whilst Crete remained under the control of Egypt and later again under the control of the Ottoman Empire until 1897. During these years, the Cretan people endured daily hardships at the hands of the occupiers, and "officially" they received very little support from the outside world. But privately Europe was sending arms and volunteers to assist the repressed people of Crete. Finally in 1897, the four great powers of England, France, Russia, and Italy occupied Crete and divided the island into four domains. It is said that on 2 November 1898, the last Ottoman soldier left Cretan soil.

But it was not until 1913, some fifteen years later, that Crete finally and officially became a part of the Greek nation. On 20 May, 1941, Crete was again occupied, this time by the German invasion during the World War II. This invasion caused terrible casualties on both sides; however, much has been written about this period of Cretan history, and suffice to say that in 1944, Germany finally withdrew its forces from Crete.

Throughout the generations, for more than four hundred years, the fierce Cretan people have been constantly subjected to both physical and emotional repression at the hands of these harsh regimes, and each regime has undoubtedly left its mark on the Cretan character and disposition.

Yet the Cretan people have managed to hold onto their native character and language throughout, which speaks volumes for their tenacity and determination of spirit. This then is the back-drop of today's Cretan men, women, and children. *But on this beautiful and fruitful island,* I ask myself, *why does there appear to be so very little or no compassion for animals and wildlife?*

After all the ancient Greeks depicted their positive relationship with their country's breed of dog, known as Alopekis, a small and fox-like canine, which is described as smart and adaptable. An intelligent little dog, who has been documented since those ancient times, can be seen on a clay vase from Thessily (circa

3000 BC), currently held in the Athens museum. These little dogs have been reported by numerous authors, including Aristotelis, and there are many artifacts portraying the ancient Greeks with their canine friends, such as an exquisite and detailed marble statue of a young boy with his pet Alopekis dog, which can be seen in the museum of Artemis Temple, Vravron, and Attica. This small Alopekis dog is thought to be the genetic forefather of the modern Maltese Bichon, of which numerous varieties can be seen on Crete today. The ancient Greek breeds were scattered all over Europe, especially the hunting dogs, as the Romans spread them everywhere they went and set up colonies. The ancient hunting dogs of Greece are very well documented, and the Cretan hound, which is a hare-hunting dog, has existed on the island of Crete since Neolithic times. This is the rarest and the most beautiful of the original Greek breeds.

Other ancient art forms depict scenes of the deceased bidding their loved ones good-bye as they entered the underworld. As these ancient art forms, sculptures, and friezes demonstrate, their loved ones were not only their family members but their dogs as well. When Odysseus returned in disguise to protect his wife Penelope from her unwelcome suitors, it is written that it was only his faithful dog Argos who recognized his master, and after waiting so long for his return, the dog then lay down at Odysseus's feet and died. When the beloved dog of Alexandra the Great fell into the sea on one of his voyages, Alexandra instructed his soldiers to dive into the sea to save his dog. Surely this also demonstrates a real bond between the ancient Greeks and their dogs and a genuine compassion and relationship between man and dog.

So what has happened in the intervening years that we now see such a change in the majority of the islanders' attitudes toward many animals and to dogs in particular? Could present-day attitudes be as a result of these people's long history of being ruled without compassion and with undoubted cruelty for more than four hundred years? If you consider the history, you will see that Crete has not yet been able to celebrate one hundred years of total independence and freedom. Only in very recent years have the people been able to live in a liberated and democratic country, and this is no time at all in the collective psyche of a nation. Could present-day attitudes be due to the very real fact that a people who are suffering and impoverished, who are having to struggle to survive in a climate of apprehension and mistrust every single day of their lives for generations, have no feelings or respect for those creatures who are even more vulnerable than themselves?

Or was it due to the influence of their Ottoman masters, and more specifically the influence of Islam, which must surely have been an overpowering one? Certainly it was enough to force numerous dedicated Christians to change their faith, at least on the surface, in order to be able to lead a half-reasonable life. I am told that before Ottoman rule came to bear down on the Cretan people, their relationship with their animals was a good one. Indeed if the early Greek references are to be believed from the observations and stories that I have mentioned, then it would be perfectly logical to assume that nothing much would have changed in the Cretan's attitude toward their animals. But from 1669 until 1897, the Cretans were under the supreme control of their Ottoman masters and Islam. We would then have found the Cretan families living as many rural families have done for generations, with their animals around them, and this scenario would most certainly not have been acceptable to their new governors.

This is not least because traditionally dogs have always been seen by Islam as impure, and the Islamic legal tradition has developed several injunctions that warn Muslims against contact with dogs. Sadly this opinion has resulted in a justification to abuse and neglect dogs wherever Islam has been the ruling power. *Hadith* is the collection of traditions about Mohammad, and these state that "Whoever keeps a dog except for the purpose of hunting, farming, or guarding of property, his reward will decrease by one *qiraat* every day." In general the average Cretan only keeps a dog for hunting, farmwork, herding, and to guard his property, this mainly applying to his chickens or sheep. Some teachings of Islam state that, "Whoever keeps a dog in the house is denied the blessings of the angels, as the angels do not enter a house in which there is a dog." Rarely do you ever find a Cretan man or woman who will allow a dog in their home. Muslims also believe that "dogs are not allowed to be a pet" because you are not allowed to touch or hold them for reasons of hygiene. They believe that Islam is the only religion in the world that is hygienic. They pray five times a day, and before prayers they must do ablutions, wash their face, feet, arms, etc., as well as washing after going to the toilet. Evidently because the dog is viewed as dirty, then contact is not compatible with their belief and traditions of cleanliness. It is believed that anything that a dog touches must be washed seven times, and one of these times it must be rubbed with soil. In my experience it is the majority of older Cretan individuals who believe that a dog is a dirty animal. They would never treat it as a pet, or show it physical affection, or allow it to sit on the furniture.

Dr. Ayoub Banderker BVMCh, a veterinary surgeon, who since 1999 has worked for organizations that primarily serve to see to the health care of animals belonging to the poor in under-privileged communities, has said that it is not *Haraam* (forbidden by the laws of Islam) to own a dog, though it is not hygienic and therefore not permissible to keep a dog in the house. This last sentence does appear to be a widely held view by many Cretan individuals. Whilst Dr. Khaled Abou El Fadl, a professor of Islamic Law at UCLA and holder of many teaching diplomas from traditional Sunni scholars in the Middle East, has come to believe that the *Hadith* (prophetic traditions) about dogs that forbid contact are fabrications. Furthermore he states that reports against dogs bear uncanny similarities to Arab folk law, leading him to suspect that someone took the tales and attributed them to the prophet Mohammed. One such belief is that when the Prophet Mohammed was hiding in a cave, it was the dogs' persistent barking that gave him away, and from that day onward, dogs were cursed, unlike the favored spider, who spun her web across the entrance of the cave where Mohammed was hiding in order to demonstrate that no one had passed inside.

Dr. Khaled Abou El Fadl also states that he was taught that dogs are impure and that black dogs in particular are considered to be evil. This is yet another belief that I have found held amongst the Cretan people. Can it be mere coincidence that so many of the Islamic teachings and laws are a part of the Cretan psyche of today? Or is it more than feasible that a people who were so oppressed for so long and who were prepared to change their religion at least on the surface in order to survive would automatically absorb the teachings and laws of Islam to a degree over time? Surely it is inevitable, if you are trying to convince your oppressors that you really have converted to Islam, you must then be prepared to demonstrate your commitment by obeying their laws.

How many generations of Cretan men, women, and children would it take for these laws, these ways of viewing the world and its animals, especially in regard to dogs, to be absorbed, especially as the average Cretan adult would not be educated enough to question or go against the basic idealism and belief that "dogs are dirty"? The total disrespect shown by parents and elders toward the innocent dog would soon be passed down from parent to child and before very long ingrained and accepted as normal behavior, as the child would not be able to recollect from where or when this opinion emanated. To inflict pain upon an animal would thus not necessarily be something to be concerned about. To acquire a dog on a whim and then to dispose of it when it was no longer of use would not be questioned. After all, there can be no respect for an animal who is believed to be *dirty*. If you cannot have a dog as a pet, nor keep it in the house, surely it is understandable that owners would not develop any feeling for dogs, as they have never bonded with animals and to do so would surely be breaking the laws of Islam.

Sadly this behavior is consistent with many people's attitudes toward dogs today. It is possible in my opinion that the repressive and often cruel Ottoman rulers, who enforced their laws of Islam on an already repressed, largely illiterate, and downtrodden people for more than four hundred years, could so easily have left a lasting legacy, which after a mere one hundred ten years is beginning to show the very early signs of change in some of the younger and better educated generation of the Cretan population. Many young Cretan individuals have told me how ashamed they feel about the way dogs are so mistreated here on Crete, and these individuals are really trying to make a difference.

But imagine how difficult this must be if you are a young child or person with a desire to help and protect animals, and yet those around you, your parents and extended family and friends, whom you have been brought up to love and respect, are telling you and showing you that you are in some way misguided and wrong. It would be a strong individual who could maintain his or her opinions and love of animals in that environment. Of course all over the world, there are individuals who are cruel to vulnerable creatures, be they children or animals, and this will probably never cease. Sadly it is a human weakness. But in many

European countries, at least there are organizations established specifically to help animals, and there are laws that are enforced to punish the perpetrators. Here on Crete there are laws, such as Greek Law 1197/1981 (article 8) and 3170/2003 (article 12). They state that "anyone who kills, abuses, or abandons animals will be punished with up to six months in prison and/or a fine ranging from three hundred to fifteen hundred euros." But sadly these laws are rarely if ever enforced. There are no equivalent animal protection organizations here on Crete, and it is generally felt that the police would not respond if they were called upon to do so. Therefore there are numerous and senseless acts of cruelty and abandonment perpetrated on a daily basis to thousands of innocent animals all over the treasured Isle of Crete.

Fourteen | First-Aid Treatment for Animals

LIVING IN CRETE is very different than living in England or America or Germany. For example, whilst we do have some very excellent vets, they may be open from 8:30 a.m. to 1:30 p.m., then they may open again in the evening from 6:00 p.m. until 9:00 p.m. That often means that there is no veterinary cover for the afternoon. Having said that, my dear George will always respond to an emergency, even when he is in the church in the middle of a baptism, as he has done for me on more than one occasion.

There is an Emergency Service Cover from Saturday noon until Monday morning, and this is covered by a rota of all the vets in each specific area of Crete, but some are not as responsive to the care of strays as others.

*The emergency telephone number for the Chania area is: 697 327 2282.

*The emergency telephone number for the Rythemnon area is: 6946 148087.

*The emergency telephone number for the Heraklion area is: 6996 566336.

This means that you really do need to have some basic knowledge of first aid if you want to be able to help any animal. The most common injuries and conditions that I have come across have been those listed below, which I will briefly cover in the section.

1. Fractured pelvis and fractures of limbs
2. Gunshot wounds
3. Dehydration and starvation
4. Burns and scalds
5. Hemorrhage
6. Epileptic seizures
7. Poisoning

1. Fractured Pelvis and Fractures of Limbs

When there are so many stray animals roaming freely on the roads, and when it is customary among some individuals to drive their unwanted animals to the national highway and then abandon them in the traffic, there is a good chance that the terrified animals will almost certainly be hit by a passing vehicle and injured or killed.

Therefore we find numerous critically injured animals with fractured legs or with the telltale scars on their hind legs that show that they have been clipped by a car's wheels, and these are the lucky ones. It is not always easy to tell if a leg is broken unless the animal has been examined by a vet and X-rayed. But one sure sign that you can look out for is *if the animal is holding the damaged limb up and he or she is reluctant to put it to the ground.*

If in doubt then, the best immediate treatment is to find a large enough box and *line it with a comfy blanket,* where the animal can be kept *safe, warm, and immobile.*

For long-term good results, it is imperative that that the fracture is treated as soon as possible. (The maximum time that treatment can be delayed is up to four days.) But it is very important that veterinary advice is sought *immediately.*

There are two main types of fracture:

Compound fracture. This is a fracture where the bone has been broken, and it can clearly be seen protruding through the skin. It is necessary that you find a sterile pad or bandage to protect the wound in order to prevent bacteria from entering the site of the injury and causing infection to the bone. It is *essential* in this case that the animal receives antibiotics *immediately,* otherwise his or her prognosis is not a good one. This type of injury can be lethal and lead to certain death

Greenstick fracture. This sort of fracture is more commonly seen in very young animals and puppies. Because the bones are still soft in young animals, they are to a degree flexible, and therefore they tend to bend rather than break (hence the name greenstick fracture). The young animal may even attempt to use the leg and to walk on it, but this should be avoided.

In all cases ensure that the animal is kept *safe, warm, and immobile* in a box that is *lined with a comfy blanket* until you can seek veterinary attention.

Fractured pelvis. In my experience I have found this to be the most common injury, especially in very young puppies, but thankfully it is also the easiest fracture to cope with.

Whilst the animal may initially be in considerable pain, they need to be placed in a *safe, warm, and comfortable box or carrying cage* that restricts unnecessary movement and from where the animal cannot escape and is safe from attack by other animals. It is essential that he or she remains there for a period of one month. You will be surprised and delighted about the excellent recovery that is made in that time.

2. Gunshot Wounds

Unfortunately one way of disposing of an unwanted dog here in Crete is to shoot it. Whilst I could never condone such a cowardly act, it would not be so bad if this was done quickly and thoroughly. Sadly only too often, this is not the case, and the dog is taken to a place where the owner thinks they will not be seen and the animal will not be found, so the dog can be shot and left for dead. But as was the situation with our dear Flipper, who was shot in the back, and with another little dog rescued very recently, called Scamp, who had been shot in the head, neither dog was killed, merely shot and then left to suffer a slow and lingering death. You may not always be able to see a wound where the shot has entered the animal's body, so do not make assumptions either way until the animal has been X-rayed. Sadly there is very little that can be done about the shot once it has entered the animal's body. The treatment and prognosis will largely depend on how quickly the animal is found and treated and of course where the shot or pellets have imbedded themselves. *Immediate and urgent treatment* should consist of *injections of steroids, vitamin B complex, and antibiotics,* so unless you are experienced with these drugs, then you will need to seek veterinary assistance *at once.* However the secondary injuries can be dealt with by you, and this treatment may enable the animal to live as normal a life as possible. The secondary injures will largely depend on where the animal was shot.

*Any obvious signs of injury, such as deep wounds will need to be regularly cleaned and kept free as possible from infection.

*It is always beneficial to administer antibiotics immediately.

Always treat any injured animal for shock.

If an animal has very pale gums, this is a good initial indicator that he or she is suffering from *shock, bleeding, or anemia.* Keep him or her in a warm and comfortable place and ensure that he or she has plenty to drink, especially if there is evidence of bleeding. Remember, any food that you give should be moist and easy to swallow (using a blender with additional water). That way if the animal is unable or unwilling to drink then he or she will be receiving the essential fluid in the food.

If the animal appears paralysed:

*He or she will need to be protected from any other animals that you may have around.

*He or she will need to be moved and turned over, as you would do with a human in the same circumstances, in order to prevent pressure sores.

*He or she will also be doubly incontinent, and it is imperative that they are kept clean and warm at all times.

I have found with a variety of animals, who have been unable to stand up, that it is beneficial if you can make them a harnesses. This can consist of a strong towel with four holes cut for the legs and tape fastened at the corners. Then the harness can be fastened above the animal, and he or she can be hoisted up, allowing his or her feet to touch the ground.

This should only be done for a few minutes at a time initially and the animal should not be left unattended.

I have always found this harness to be extremely beneficial, and I have used it successfully on dogs, cats, and sheep. It enables the animals' circulation to be improved, and it also seems to help to retrain them. It also appears to serve to remind them that they are able to walk when their feet feel the ground beneath them, thus giving the animals renewed confidence and a desire to do even more. When we found Flipper, he had no feeling or movement in his back legs, and they merely trailed behind him. Once in the wheels, he seemed to be able to feel the ground, and he eventually began to move his legs as if he were walking. Now when he travels at top speeds, he is also able to raise his feet from the ground and to hold them in the air. At times he uses them to kick off with to increase his speed in his chariot.

Whatever the injuries are, do not be disheartened, progress can be slow, but the rewards for patience and constant good nursing care are *enormous.*

3. Dehydration and Starvation

The majority of puppies and dogs that are found during the hot summer months are thirsty and dehydrated, as there may not have been any rain for several months. Therefore there are no pools of rainwater to quench their thirst and no street fountains or garden pools available, as they might otherwise find in England, America, or Germany. But thirst is one thing, and dehydration is much more serious, leading to kidney damage and heart failure. A volunteer and I found one such dog (Leukos), who was chained to a building, and the owner had forgotten to give him any food or water for several days. Or else he intended to just ignore him and leave him to die, as he was no longer needed. When we found this poor animal, he was unable to get up, and he was so very weak that he was barely able to raise his head from the ground. Our first impression was that maybe he had been involved in an accident until we looked around the surrounding area where he was fastened and realized that there was no evidence that he had been given any food or water. We carried the animal to the car and brought him to my place. He obviously wanted to drink copious amounts of fluid, but this is not advisable.

Initial treatment should consist of giving the animal small and frequent amounts of fluid, any warm liquid, such as water or milk mixed with glucose, sugar, or honey. Within a few days, Leukos recovered completely and now he lives happily with the volunteer who found him.

Starvation. When we find a starving animal, our instinct is to give him or her a huge bowl of food, but this is not advisable. If you are able to prepare well–cooked, white, boiled rice and chicken, than this is an ideal meal and should be offered initially in very small quantities several times a day. I have frequently found starving dogs who have never eaten branded dog food in their lives, and even though they are hungry, they may well refuse it. The most common food that animals are given here in Crete is *bread,* and this may be the only food that the animal has ever tasted in his or her entire life. In these cases I have often spent many weeks feeding such an animal on bread after first spreading it with multivitamin creams and very small amounts of dog meat until the animal is willing to accept the new food.

Never give any animal (unless it is a calf) cow's milk, especially very young puppies, as in my experience this has a detrimental effect on the lining of the stomach, and it can cause long-term problems and diarrhea. You can safely give them the Noy Noy tinned milk diluted, *half milk* and *half water.* The one that is suitable for children is ideal.

4. Burns and Scalds

Many animals are subjected to nonaccidental burns and scalds here in Crete. Angry tavern owners who wish to discourage an animal may throw a pan of boiling water over it. Children can find it amusing to spray an unsuspecting animal with lighter fuel or other aerosols and then to set it alight.

Treatment. First soak the burned or scalded area *immediately* with freezing-cold water; ice cubes in bag can be placed on the burning area, and even bags of frozen vegetables could be applied if that is all you have available (as the dog's coat tends to hold the heat and therefore continue the burning process until the heat can be reduced).

*Trim the hair off from the burned and surrounding area *immediately*.

*Keep the animal warm and quiet and away from other animals and treat for shock.

*Do not wash the wound or spray with an antiseptic spray, as this will be extremely painful.

*Cover the area with sterile gauze, preferably one specifically impregnated with antibiotic and steroid crèmes, as this helps with the healing process.

**It is *essential* that you use a cream on the sterile gauze to prevent it sticking to the wound.

Blisters may occur; even with an open wound, it is very important not to burst these or allow them to get infected.

Treating such an injured animal here in Crete in the open air can be quite problematic. I had one such animal who I cared for on my verandah during the one of hottest months of the year. I positioned him on a white sheet, which was frequently replaced in order to keep his surrounding area as clean as possible.

To prevent the numerous flies from attacking his open wounds, I rubbed neat citronella oil into the remaining *unburned* areas of his body, and this prevented any flies and insects from contaminating the nearby open wounds.

I have also found lavender to be an excellent fly repellent.

5. Hemorrhage

There are two most common types of haemorrhage:

Bleeding from a vein. This is the most common type, as the veins are the blood vessels that are closest to the surface of the skin. Whilst there can appear to be a lot of blood, it is usually darker in color, and it is often relatively easy to control as it *flows out* rather than spurts out. This is seldom life threatening, and in a healthy dog this should soon stop.

Bleeding from an artery. This is less common because arteries are stronger than veins and are not so close to the surface of the skin. However *arterial hemorrhage* is much more serious. The blood is bright red, and it tends to spurt out rather than flow, and therefore it is much more difficult to stop.

Treatment for both types is to apply pressure to the area until you can reach a vet and to bandage with plenty of padding. If the hemorrhaging is from the animal's limbs, then attempt to keep the injured limb elevated. Keep the animal immobilized, quiet, and warm, and treat him or her for shock and encourage him or her to drink water.

Seek veterinary assistance immediately.

6. Epileptic Seizures

Puppy fits are not very common, but they can be associated with roundworm infestations in a puppy. The books will tell you that they are mainly transient in nature; however, they can be rather frightening for both the carer and the puppy, and it is always wise to contact a veterinary surgeon. The puppy can appear to be overexcited and hyperactive just before a fit, and he or she may well fall down. His eyes may appear glazed, and he may froth at the mouth and even look as if he is snarling at you. Whilst experiencing a fit, the puppy may also appear to snap at the carer. His muscles will twitch, and his legs may appear to be paddling.

Treatment. Stay calm and as encouraging as you are *able*. If you are unable to do this, then place the dog in a safe environment, preferably in a dark and quiet area until the fit appears to have stopped. The main aim in any fit is to ensure that the animal is safe and cannot hurt himself or be hurt by other animals and that the fits are stopped as soon as possible to avoid any possible brain damage. If you have any sedative, such as Valium suppositories, then you could use them, and administer rectally, but obviously you cannot give anything orally whilst the puppy is fitting.

In my experience a puppy has never suffered only one fit, and therefore the main aim is to seek medical assistance and to keep him or her calm and sedated if possible.

Epilepsy. This is not very often found in dogs under the age of eighteen months. If a mature dog suffers from epilepsy, the seizures often occur at regular intervals, i.e. weekly, monthly, or even annually. Once a dog has been diagnosed as epileptic, this tends to be a diagnosis for life.

A dog having an epileptic fit will usually froth at the mouth, the muscles may twitch, and he will fall down, the symptoms appearing much the same as described above in puppy fits.

Your dog may empty his bladder and bowel, which he or she is unaware of. He could become unconscious and seem unable to recognise you.

Any seizure can last from a few seconds to ten minutes or more, and afterward your dog will appear dazed, confused, and a little frightened. The whole experience, when it first happens, can be equally scary for both the dog and the carer, but do not despair. I have come across many dogs who lead an otherwise full and active life with the correct medication, which can be prescribed through the veterinary.

7. Poisoning

Animals can be poisoned by a variety of substances, some of which may not be so obvious. See list below of just a few.

- Anti-inflammatory drugs—aspirin, ibuprofen, etc.
- Paracetamol
- Vitamin D—contained within creams for psoriasis or other skin conditions (normally chewed by puppies)
- Weed killers—ant killers insecticidal sprays, wood worm treatments
- Dark chocolate

- Slug bait
- Alcohol
- Disinfectants
- Antifreeze
- Rat poison (see notes on poisoning in Crete)

It is always best to try to identify the type of poison if you can and contact your veterinary surgery immediately. However this is not always possible, especially here in Crete. So if this is not an option, then the following basic first aid can be given at home.

Please first consider the warnings below.

1. If *under* four hours since the poison was ingested you can *induce vomiting* using *two teaspoons of mustard in a cup of warm water.*

2. If *after* four hours, you can give a mild laxative to speed up the rate in which the intestines will reject the substance and therefore limit its reabsorption into the body.

3. *Wash any contaminated skin.*

4. *Give the antidote if you have it available.*

Warnings.

- *Do not induce vomiting* if the poison is suspected to be corrosive, such as disinfectant solutions, strong acids, bleach, etc.
- *Do not induce vomiting* to an unconscious or fitting animal. Collapsed animals can inhale their vomit.

- ■ *Do not use salt* to induce vomiting as this will cause severe electrolyte imbalances, which could be more harmful.
- ■ *Do not induce vomiting* if the poison has been ingested for more than *four hours* previously.

Poisoning in Crete. It is recommended that due to the high number of poisoning cases here where rodenticides, i.e. rat bait, are used that the following procedure is followed. You can purchase the drug from your vet called Fitalon (apomorphine) and make a note, with advice from your vet, as to how much to give your own animal. This can be stored in a dark place for many years if it is not opened.

You can purchase a drug from the pharmacy called atropine. This is an antidote to most of the poisoning cases in Crete. *But please be aware that this drug can do more harm if administered with the wrong poison, so you must try to speak to a vet before using it.*

In an emergency if less than four hours, give the amount of Fitalon required by injection *under the skin,* and this will cause vomiting (even if the animal is already vomiting).

Dosage. 0.1 to 0.6 ml per 10 kg of body weight.

Contact your vet and report the symptoms.

Only administer the atropine after speaking to a vet. But if you are really unable to contact a vet, *first check the dog's pupils. If they are large, i.e., dilated, then do not give atropine. If they are small, i.e., pinpoint, or normal, you may give one or two vials for every 10 kg of the dog's body weight.*

Fifteen | Support Groups on Crete

THROUGHOUT THIS BOOK I have made reference to the majority of the rescued dogs who we care for travelling to their new families and homes in Germany. Ever since we arrived on Crete, there has been a great deal of gossip and rumor emerging from time to time right across the island regarding the many German groups who not only support me but others like me, who are doing the same valuable work here. The fact is that the German population donate a great deal of money and have been doing so for many years toward helping animals, not only on Crete but on other Greek islands, and indeed all over the world where the abuse of animals is prevalent. Not only do they send us the much-needed Euros to aid us in our work, but they send some very experienced and extremely hardworking veterinarians like Ines, who has worked courageously to ease the plight and suffering of so many animals all over this island and indeed all over the world. Without the dedication of these vets and without these groups and their financial support, none of the animal protection groups like myself could continue with the work that we do. The Cretan authorities do not welcome or agree to these organizations working here, which in my opinion is a great shame, as many animals go untreated because of financial restraints and because individuals are reluctant to pay for the treatment of an animal that is not their own.

The majority of rumors that I have come across say that the animals of Crete are sent to Germany for vivisection or to be used in medical experimentation. Surely this would be a very expensive way for the German organizations to acquire their material for any experimentation; it would be cheaper and a lot easier to acquire such animals from within Germany. To be able to carry out any drug or medical research on animals, anyone with any experience in these matters will tell you that laboratories require "pure" animals bred for that specific purpose and identical enough in type and breed so their results can be validated. No one can possibly say or be sure of what conglomeration of diseases and infections, or what sort of parasites, any one of the poor rescued animals of Crete may have had in their systems at one time or another or even what diseases they may have inherited from their parents.

Therefore I cannot imagine any scientific results being worth a dime if they were reliant on the animals of Crete.

Whenever these absurd rumors raise their ugly heads, I always confront the speaker and request that they provide me with some material evidence in the shape of newspaper articles, videos, or the details of where the information has emanated from. Despite my numerous requests, no one has ever been able to provide me with one small shred of evidence to substantiate these rumors. But what I do have in my possession are hundreds of photographs of happy, healthy, and clearly much-loved dogs, whom I can see playing in the gardens of their new homes in Germany, France, England, Denmark, Finland, and Switzerland, or attending their German puppy training schools wearing little kerchiefs around their necks. When they came to me, these puppies and dogs were often sick and injured or had been abandoned on the national roads, some of them too young to be able to fend for themselves, some even as young as a few hours old when they were found.

So allow me to tell you how it all works for me. Every puppy or dog who I care for is initially placed in isolation for a period of two weeks. This period should ideally be much longer, but limited space and isolation areas often prevent this. Each animal is treated immediately for both internal and external parasites. This is extremely important, as even just a few fleas can cause severe anemia and death in small puppies. When I am sure that they do not appear to have any illness or gastric problems, then they are taken to the vet for their first vaccination to guard them against Parvovirus-Distemper-Hepatitis-Leptospirosis, and once they are over the age of three months, they can also have a vaccination against rabies. These vaccinations, with the exception of the rabies vaccine, are repeated after four weeks. As long as these vaccinations have been carried out within the appropriate time scales, the animal is free to travel to Germany, Denmark, France, Finland, and Switzerland. (Please note that further procedures need to be observed for some other European countries such as Norway, Sweden, and England, and you would need to contact your vet or the embassy of the relevant country.) These vaccinations are then required to be given at one-year intervals throughout the animal's life.

When a female dog has had her first season, which usually occurs after she is six months old, we prepare to neuter her to ensure that there will be no more puppies. Male dogs are castrated a little later to allow for their growth to be completed.

Whilst all these procedures are being carried out, we take photographs of the dogs and place them on the Web site of Grenzenlose Tierliebe. But there are hundreds of doggy portals on the Internet where this can be done. Interested families in Europe are then able to browse, and if they find a dog that they feel would be suitable for them, they can contact the source.

In theory anyone can re-home a dog in this manner. But from our point of view, we work very closely with all the German groups that support us and who we can trust, thereby ensuring that we know exactly where each and every one of our beloved animals goes. Grenzenlose Tierliebe checks out the owners in their homes prior to the dog arriving in Germany in an attempt to ensure that our dogs and puppies get the best opportunities that we can offer them.

Arche Noah Kreta also re-homes some of our precious animals. Generally they place them in small, private animal shelters or foster homes. Then interested families must visit the animal on at least three occasions during which time the staff are able to interview them and assess their interaction with the dog or puppy of their choice.

Currently there are four separate Animal Protection Groups who assist me with my work. They all work in very different ways, but all are essential to me and other animal protectors on the island of Crete in the work that they do, and without each group's unique and individual continual support, none of us could not continue with the work.

I have asked each group to write a little bit about their organizations, using their own words, so you have an idea about their work, ensuring that our Cretan dogs and other animals receive the best that we can offer them and surely what every animal is entitled to in this life. Of course no one is so stupid as to assume that every single dog goes to the perfect home and there they live happily ever after. But we all do our best to ensure that the homes the dogs do go to are as good as we can get, and after all is said and done, I tend to think that even a less-than-perfect home in one of these European countries has to be better than a life tied to a freezing-cold metal barrel in winter by a six-inch chain, surrounded by their own excrement day after day with no food or water for days at a time, no medical assistance, and no love. Or to be left to die slowly after being shot in the back or the head, as in the cases of our dear Flipper or our newest resident Scamp and then to be left in an isolated municipal garbage dump or at the side of the road . . . or to be poisoned or to be thrown from a moving vehicle onto a busy main road . . . or even to be hung like a criminal in elder times—these are just some of the deaths that await so many of our dear Cretan animals at the hands of individuals who dare to call themselves human beings.

1. Arche Noah Kreta

This was the first German organization that I came across on Crete. They had taken possession of the old Cretan animal shelter, which was in a terrible condition prior to their involvement, as it had been used merely to deposit all the stray dogs from the roads with no supervision or care being offered to them.

Arche Noah was established in1997, and they came to Crete in order set up neutering programs across the entire island and to offer medical support to the existing animal protection groups. Their aim was to neuter as many animals as possible in order to prevent the future unborn generations from suffering the injuries, starvation, and poisonings Arche Noah witnessed. As well as this, they carried out numerous surgical operations to improve the health of the current population of animals, for example, treating infected eyes and damaged limbs, removing tumours, and repairing the injuries caused by man's cruelty. Sadly this group was forced to leave Crete, but they still continue to help the various organizations whenever they can, both on Crete and in other parts of the world.

For example, they will take a severely injured or sick animal to Germany where it can be treated and re-homed afterward. Arche Noah Kreta will pay for these expenses, and every year they take between one hundred fifty and two hundred injured and sick animals for such treatment. They also take healthy dogs, which have been abandoned on Crete, to Germany for re-homing to loving families, as they tell me that German families love the gentle and sociable nature of these Cretan dogs.

Every year Arche Noah Kreta sends between eighty and one hundred tons of food to Crete to help all the various groups feed the many abandoned animals we are caring for. They also send a sum of money every month to six animal protection groups on the island to support their various projects, which are first agreed upon by their committee.

2. Grenzenlose Tierlebe

I met Ilona and Thomas Bauemeister in June 2007 after they contacted me regarding taking two dogs back that they had found to Germany. Since that time, Ilona explains adequately what our relationship has been and how many dogs she and her husband Thomas have re-homed in Germany from our place. This work is not easy, as Ilona and Thomas are meticulous in their search for the right family for the right dog. It is an expensive and time-consuming procedure, as they often travel hundreds of kilometers across Germany so they can visit and check out any potential family and its individual members for our beloved dogs and puppies, for which we are all forever grateful. They not only attempt to find as perfect a home as they are able for the dogs and puppies, but they also offer the new owners continuous support and advice throughout the life of their adopted pet. Who could ask for more?

* * *

Our first stay on Crete was in the year 2007, which was meant to be a rest from animal protection for my husband and myself. But whilst we were staying on Crete, we found two dogs who were living in dreadful and miserable conditions and in desperate need of our help if they were to survive. We were given the telephone number of Freida and Colin, who immediately offered to help us, which touched us very much and for which we will always be thankful. Freida and Colin instantly offered these two sweethearts a foster home whilst they could be prepared to travel to Germany. This meant them having the necessary vaccinations, a microchip, and a European passport. They were also castrated so they would be ready to make the journey to our home. In Germany meanwhile, we were already trying to find them good and permanent homes. About two months later we returned to Crete so we could take the two dogs back with us. Once we were back in Germany again, we knew that we wanted to support Freida and Colin in their animal protection work on Crete and to help to ease the suffering of the numerous animals. By the end of May 2007, we were able to organize our first delivery of donations to Crete. The biggest part of this delivery was the urgently needed food. At the same time, through our organization, we established our re-homing program for the rescued dogs from Crete.

In June 2007 the first sweethearts traveled from Crete to Germany and were placed in their lovely homes where they could stay forever. Since that time in the last two years, we have been able to find more than one hundred wonderful and caring homes for the abandoned Cretan dogs. It is very important for us that these homes really are long-term. They must be good and caring families or individuals with whom these dogs can spend their entire lives. That is one reason why we visit every single home. We insist on meeting all the family members personally before we allow the re-homing process to go ahead. Even after the re-homing, we feel that it is very important for us to keep in regular contact with everyone who has adopted one of our dogs. We want to remain as their partner and their friend, someone who they can always turn to if they have any problems with any of our dogs for the animal's entire life, and we do our utmost to address any difficulties that may arise. This way we are assured that both the owner and our precious animals are happy.

From the start of our re-homing program on Crete, we have paid for the dogs fly to their new homes in Germany during the winter season when there are no direct flights with German airlines to Crete. The flights at this time, i.e. from the end of October until the end of April, with the Greek airlines are very expensive as the dogs have to travel cargo. This means that the traveling costs are charged by the dog's weight and the weight of the traveling box. Unfortunately for us, this is always very costly for our organization, even for the very small dogs. But we feel that the offer of a good home is too good to miss when there are always so many lovely dogs in need. During the summer season, which is from the beginning of May until the end of October, we are therefore very grateful for every offer of a flying partnership, as the traveling costs are much cheaper.

Our entire commitment and engagement in Greece, France, and Germany is 100% honorary, which means that from every euro we get as a donation, the animals in need benefit directly and entirely from the full amount. The yearly membership fee in our organization is thirty Euros, and we are always happy to welcome every new member! If you would like to get a brief view of our everyday life with animals, we invite you to visit our Web site: www.grenzenlose-tierliebe.de.

Grenzenlose Tierliebe is one of the few organizations in Germany that does not make any distinction between wild animals and so-called domestic animals that we feel are unfortunately used and exploited by and for human beings. We therefore live our lives without using any animal products. We decided in the middle of the year 2008, after nearly twenty years of following a vegan diet, to change to a vegan-raw food diet, which we have practiced successfully and which gives us the optimal health and energy for our commitment and work with animal protection.

We would like to thank Freida and Colin for their wonderful and trustworthy work together with us, and we sincerely hope that many interested people will read Freida's book, which is to be sold in the aid of animal protection on Crete. Many greetings from the bottom of our hearts, to all friends of animals around the world.

Your Ilona and Thomas Baumeister

3. Kreta Tierhilfe

Whilst Kreta Tierhilfe is a newly formed group, its committee and founding fathers have been involved in animal protection for many years. Their aims are to support our work and animal protectors on Crete in whatever way they are able.

By sending us regular financial support, we are able to buy food and materials, and it also assists us with the payment of veterinary bills and neutering of stray and injured animals who are not re-homed by Grenzenlose Tierliebe. It also helps us to pay for the costly treatment of internal and external parasites, which is never-ending due to the warmer climate here on Crete. Kreta Tierhilfe has also assisted us with the much-needed medication that has enabled our very elderly donkey to walk again and to pay for medical treatment and vaccinations, especially for the many cats and the disabled dogs who we care for that can never be re-homed in Germany, and so they need to remain with us for their entire lives.

Kreta Tierhilfe financial help enables us to help other sick and injured animals who we know of and who may require veterinary help that their owners are unable to provide, such as enabling us to purchase the anti-tetanus vaccine for the village donkeys, so we never repeat the dreadful episode two Christmases ago, which you can read about in Christmas Tails, when we tried but sadly failed to save the life of a local village donkey who was suffering from tetanus. After that tragic episode, we then made a commitment to vaccinate the local village donkeys in order to prevent this agonizing death ever happening again to any of the others.

Trying to care for so many neglected and abandoned animals is expensive as there are so many hidden costs, such as the extra water and electricity used for the daily cleaning of kennels and blankets. The numerous trips to the veterinary clinic and phone calls that have to be made are just a few examples, and without this group's support, we could not continue with the work. Kreta Tierhilfe also tries to encourage their members to commit to a regular monthly amount of money for a specific animal who needs our long-term care, and they then become that animal's foster parent. In addition some of their members also send us regular parcels of very useful items for the animals.

The organization believes that German people in general feel a high social responsibility for animals all over the world and that they are not prepared or willing to accept the misery that the majority of animals of Crete have to suffer on a daily basis. They believe that some individuals join their organization and want to get involved in particularly helping the animals of Crete because they have visited the island on holiday, and they have seen for themselves the suffering of the animals who live here. For the chairman, it is because he was working on Crete for many years, and he saw the abject misery and cruelty for himself on a daily basis.

You may contact them at Kreta Tierhilfe at 1 Vorsitzender. Dieter Fischer Norderatrasse 20 24848 Kropp, Germany. Telephone: 0049(0)4624 8688. Fax: 0049(0)4624 517080. E-mail: FischerKropp@aol.com. Or go their Web site, which is www.Kreta-Tierhilfe.eu

4. Greek Animal Welfare Fund

The Greek Animal Welfare Fund (G.A.W.F.) was founded in 1959. It is a non-profit organization in both Greece and the U.K. with over fifty years of action for animals in Greece.

Working with animal welfare groups. One of G.A.W.F.'s principal activities is providing financial assistance to organizations undertaking animal welfare work in Greece. This has included support for neutering programs, care for stray animals, assistance to shelters and hospitals, protection of wildlife, and educational campaigns.

I became aware of this organization about four years ago when I applied for a grant to enable me to carry out a program for neutering stray cats. Sadly, this program ceased when the demand for the service far outweighed our financial capabilities.

Neutering. In addition to awarding grants toward neutering programs, G.A.W.F. visits islands and rural areas that have no veterinary practice to carry out veterinary programs. Approximately one hundred animals are spayed and castrated during an average four-day program.

Equines. G.A.W.F. is working on practical ways of improving the welfare for Greece's working donkeys, horses, and mules. The G.A.W.F. team consists of an equine vet, farrier, and equine dentist. In addition to treating the animals, local people receive instruction on equine care. Training of Greek vets and individuals interested in hoof care and dental procedures have received specialist training in the U.K. G.A.W.F. also publishes a range of educational material, including a book on donkey care, leaflets on various equine care, and a video on shoeing. I have experienced this wonderful service when the equine team was on Crete three years ago and they visited us and the local donkeys in the village of Armenio. This is something they have continued to do on an annual basis, and the service has proven to be invaluable to us, especially with a donkey we acquired who was unable to walk. With the equine team's specialist help, he improved tremendously and lived a pleasant retirement until the time came when his condition again deteriorated and he needed to be euthanized. Thankfully Elisa from the team was able to discuss the procedure with my vet George, which then enabled him to carry it out, enabling our donkey to die peacefully and with the dignity he so deserved.

Education. Since the education program began in January 1997, G.A.W.F. has visited schools all over Greece, giving lessons to thousands of students annually. Since 1998 G.A.W.F. has organized an annual writing competition called "Once Upon an Animal." The competition attracts over six thousand entries each year from all over the country.

Public awareness. G.A.W.F. produces leaflets and posters on various animal welfare issues, including responsible pet ownership, neutering, and the care of equines. G.A.W.F. is also active in the media, sending out regular press releases relating to a wide range of animal welfare issues.

Lobbying. G.A.W.F. plays an active role in lobbying for improvements of animal welfare laws, including legislation pertaining to companion animals, farm animals, working animals, pet shops, importation of wild-caught exotics, circuses with performing animals, and zoo animals. In addition, G.A.W.F. applies pressure at national and local government levels with regard to enforcement of existing animal welfare legislation.

The End

Lightning Source UK Ltd.
Milton Keynes UK
05 December 2009

147164UK00001B/15/P